THE
VEDIC PHILOSOPHY

THE VEDIC PHILOSOPHY

OR AN EXPOSITION OF THE SACRED AND MYSTERIOUS MONOSYLLABLE

ॐ

ओम् AUM

THE MANDUKYA UPANISHAD (TEXT)
WITH
ENGLISH TRANSLATION, COMMENTARY
AND
AN INTRODUCTION
BY

HAR NARAYANA
(Late Home Minister Kashmir State)

SECOND REVISED AND ENLARGED EDITION

COSMO PUBLICATIONS
2000 INDIA

The Vedic Philosophy

First COSMO Print 2000

ISBN 81-7020-971-4

Published by
MRS. RANI KAPOOR
for COSMO PUBLICATIONS Div. of
GENESIS PUBLISHING PVT. LTD.
24-B, Ansari Road,
Darya Ganj,
New Delhi-110 002, INDIA

Printed at
Mehra Offset Press

सर्वेषामपि चैतेषां शुभानामिह कर्मणाम् ।
किञ्चिच्छ्रेयस्करतरं कर्मोक्तं पुरुषं प्रति ॥ ८४ ॥
सर्वेषामपि चैतेषामात्मज्ञानं परं स्मृतम् ।
तद्ध्यग्र्यं सर्वविद्यानां प्राप्यते ह्यमृतं ततः ॥ ८५ ॥

84. "Among all those good acts performed in this world, said the sages, is no single act held more powerful than the rest in leading men to beatitude" ?

85. "Of all those duties, answered Bhrigu, the principal is to acquire (from the *Upanishads*) *a true Knowledge of Self* (*the Real Entity*) ; that is the most exalted of all sciences, because it ensures immortality."

Manu Simriti, Chapter XII.

EXTRACTS FROM COMMENTS IN PAPERS AND OPINIONS.

THE above work. . . . will be found very useful to all who desire to acquaint themselves with the fundamental principles of Eastern philosophy and Metaphysics. The introduction . . . . evinces much subtle analysis and familiarity with metaphysical reasoning. . . . . . The monosyllable, Aum, is analysed and discussed at great length, much light being thrown upon the different aspects of this sacred root word. . . . The ideas are clearly put, without useless Verbiage . . . .

—*The Theosophist* (*Madras*), November 1895.

. . . . Lala Har Nârâyana has spared no pains to make the Commentary as full and lucid as possible. The introduction is wholly his own and is a careful examination of Vedantic Philosophy with parallel lines of thought of European Philosophers.

—*The Tribune* (*Lahore*), 11th December 1895.

. . . . The book contains many valuable hints and new ideas which can be of great use to a beginner. The book can repay perusal. We therefore recommend it to our fellow countrymen.

—*The Arya Patrika* (*Lahore*), 21st December 1896.

The book is not only useful to our countrymen who wish to become theists instead of becomming atheists and agnostics but also to the English people who wish to know the Ancient Aryan mysterous Monosyllable (Aum).

—*The Crescent*, September 1896.

The disquisition of "Aum" contained in the book is a very able one and we recommend the book to all Aryâs. The Library of every Ârya Samâj should have a copy of it.

—*The Agra Advertiser*, 16th March 1897.

. . . . . The work, which we have no doubt in pronouncing to be a very honest and satisfactory one, especially in these days of hasty and irresponsible "book-building." The Māndūkya Upanishad is very closely translated and the notes are very useful. *The book is on the whole a very valuable one and deserves to be in the hands of all students of the Vedânta.*

It throws a considerable light on a number of points and contains many precious extracts from the Upanishads, simply and accurately rendered. The general phylosophy of *Aum* has been beautifully and succinctly explained. and its orthography minutely examined. The writer appears to be a respectable Upanishadic scholar and to have had *Kramavichârnâ*, that is, regular enquiry in the proper orthodox fashion, and deserves to be congratulated on the production of a really useful book. . . . .

—*The Awakened India, Madras,* April 1897.

In fact the little book of Har Nârâyana is a good explanation of the Vedic Religion as it is usually known.

From this point of view the author has fully attained his object and the western Idea particularly cannot but be grateful to him for his work.

LE LOTUS BLEU.

PARIS, *May* 1896.

For students of the Eastern philosophy who approach the study from the western standpoint, a most useful aid will be found in "The Vedic Philosophy."

The author has studied Herbert Spencer and shows how the Vedic philosophy while accepting his (Spencer's) arguments in regard to ultimate truths, demurs to his conclusion—that ultimates are in their nature unknowable.

We strongly recommend this work to all Theosophists.

THEOSOPHY IN AUSTRALIA.

SYDNEY, 11*th April* 1896.

From this small extract you will be able to see that the work announced here is an important one well worth reading for those who are not entirely unacquainted with that what it speaks of and therefore can well recommend same.

AMSTERDAM, *October* 1896. THEOSOPHIA.

. . . . It is a Unique and original work and its author deserves the thanks of all religiously disposed educated Hindus. The work is highly instructive and the expositions and explanations given in it testify to the master mind of its author and help the reader in understanding and appreciating the cardinal doctrines of Hindu religion.

GOPAL CHANDRA SIRKAR S'ASTRI, M. A., B. L.

20, Mirzapur Lane, *Vakil, High Court, Calcutta.*

CALCUTTA, *25th February* 1896.

Although I had, the opportunity of reading only a few pages of the book, it appeared very interesting to me and to contain some ideas which seemed to me original and striking. . . . . Allow me, however, to offer my best thanks for the book which I can already say is very thoughtful.

PRAMADA DAS MITTER.

BENARES, *27th February* 1896.

The notes appended to the text often contain rare and interesting information, while the preface is a master-piece of close reasoning and lucid exposition. The book shows that you have studied Vedânta carefully and possess the power of expressing your ideas in a clear, forcible language. The disquisition on "AUM" contained in the book is a very able one and will be read with interest even by those who do not believe in the views set forth in it.

RAJENDRA CHANDRA SASTRI, M. A.,
Premchand Roychand Scholar,
Librarian Government, Bengal

BENGAL LIBRARY, *7th August* 1896.

The first part of your book containing an exposition of the mysterious syllable *"Aum"* forms a very good introduction to Vedic Philosophy or Vedantism as it is generally called.

The second part may be considered as a supplement to Part I. The English translation of the 12 aphorisms of the Mândukya Upanishad which it contains is as remarkable for its lucidity and fidelity as the notes appended to it are approprite and erudite.

NILMANI MUKERJEE, M.A., B.L.,
Principal, Sanskrit College, Calcutta.

CALCUTTA, 18*th March* 1896.

. . . . . I have great pleasure in stating that the essays are very suggestive and some of the attempts at defining philosophy and adopting it to modern European views. The work does very great credit to your industry and research and I hope you will follow it up by fresh publications.

THE HONORABLE M. G. RANADE,
BOMBAY, 5*th March* 1896. *Judge, High Court, Bombay.*

Shri Swâmi Shankarâchârya of the Shârda Pith (Dwârkâ) praised at great length in Sanskrit as to the importance of the work and observed that it contained the essence of all the Upanishads and Vedânta.

CAMP JULLUNDUR, *June* 1896.

Several Europeans have endeavoured to present to the world expositions of Indian philosophies and without in any way detracting from the value of their labours, surely no one has done better than Har Nârâyana who, being himself a Vedântin, is qualified to give such information as will enable students to arrive at just conclusions with reference to the subjects upon which his work treats.

Aucland (Newzeland) 27-10-96. W. H. DRAFFIN.

Thank you for your book which appears to me to show a good deal of research and has much of interest in it.

. . . .

BANGALORE 16-10-95. W. M. YOUNG, M. A., K. C. S. I.

I am desired by Mr. Herbert Spencer to convey his thanks for the Copy of your work on *Vedic Philosophy* which you have been good enough to send him.

With regard to your request for an expression of opinion on your criticisms I am to say that compliance is out of the question. Mr. Spencer is an invalid and is unable. . . . .

LONDON, *27th March* 1897. TROUGHTON.

"I may say if you will allow me that I know no book that has so much value for me. I have had it now about five years and often read it. There is nothing of this sort in English literature; and what there is of a transcendental nature is so wordy as to be of little value. Most writers think to be heard for their much speaking and so their mighty tunes make good furniture but little thought, yours is free of such faults. The argument is well reasoned, the logic is good and the language is simple and this I say in appreciation.—*Charles H. Spencer, Thornfield, Parlington, Manchester, England,* 4th January 1906.

"Let me say again that your book has been more appreciated by me than any book I have or have read. I say this deliberately with no intention to flatter, not for its style or logic but simply for its contents, and it finds me accepting your position almost without reserve. Of course I am well acquainted with most of the publications upon Eastern Philosophy and thought obtainable here and the literature of the Theosophic Society. As a theory your position is unassailable.—*Charles H. Spencer,* 28th March 1906.

CONTENTS.

PREFACE.

SALUTATIONS to my spiritual preceptor Bâwâ Naginâ Singh, Atamadarshi, of Phagwârâ. Through his teachings conviction was brought to my mind of the real nature of things and my ignorance of Self was removed.

This book was written in 1891 and at the request of several of my friends, I printed it for the benefit of the seekers after truth.

I hope the reader will charitably give his attention to the thoughts and the subject-matter contained in these pages, and overlook literary defects, it any.

I am thankful to Babu Rai Baroda Kanth Laheri, F.T.S., &c., of Ludhiana and to my friend, Mr. George Hay of Jullundur, for their kindness in reading the manuscript, and suggesting corrections which have been of much value. My thanks are also due to my friends Lalas Sri Gopal and Mulchand, and to my cousin, Lala Shib Charan Das, B.A., for their general help.

SIMLA,
The 15th June, 1895.

HAR NÂRÂYANA.

PREFACE TO THE NEW REVISED EDITION 1919.

This book has been out of print for the last twenty years and the ever increasing calls have obliged me to bring out a new edition. In doing so, I have found it necessary to revise and enlarge some portions without in any way materially altering the substance of the text.

SIMLA,
OMKÂRA COTTAGE,
The 15th October, 1919.

NOTE.

á or â denotes the sound of a as in Alms, Calm &c.

e or é	„	„	„	e as of a in fate, rate &c.
I'	„	„	„	I as of ee, in feet, meet &c.
S'	„	„	„	S as of 'sh' in shut, shore &c.

ओम्.

INTRODUCTION.

Preamble.

THE questions that first arise in the mind of an enquirer after truth are generally of the nature discussed in this treatise. A few short explanatory notes given here will form an introduction.

Vedântic method of teaching Philosophy.

If the ultimate truths of Philosophy, which ordinary commonsense will neither admit nor comprehend, be at once told to a beginner, he will most assuredly be confused, and will probably give up their study with disgust. But if a wise teacher, after gauging the acquirements and capabilities of his pupil, steadily and slowly instructs him and removes his errors by leading him on to higher truths, the pupil at last comes to believe in truths which he would strongly have opposed, had they been told to him all at once. The Vedânta Philosophy always recommends a slow and sure method of instruction, and it is, therefore, no wonder that those who have not carefully and patiently studied it, quite erroneously believe it to be self-contradictory and misleading. The system of Vedântic Philosophy assumes, as a matter of fact, at the outset, things as they are, and then exposes the illusions which external appearances create in the mind of a beginner.

I. Evolution and Involution of the World.

Pursuing the method mentioned above, let us begin to think with an enquirer, whether the world existed as it is from eternity. A little reflection and careful observation will show that every thing around us, including our own body and mind is undergoing a change—that in the course of time that which was unmanifest becomes manifest and the manifest in course of time disappears and again becomes unmanifest. This changeableness excites within us a desire for enquiry.

as to what undergoes all this change. By an analysis of the things of this world, as taught in the Vedânta Philosophy, we find that all objects are included in the five primary elements called Prithvi (Solids), Apas (Liquids), Tejas (Heat), Vâyu (Gases) and Akâsha (Ether). Enquiry pushed a little further shows that we do not find any of these elements in their simple and pure state. Whatsoever we see, we find it a mixture of all the five elements; for instance, the Solids contain one half of the element of Prithvi (Solidity), and the other half consists of a proportionate part of the rest of the elements. Likewise is the case with the liquids and the other elements.* We can think of a simple element, but we cannot actually perceive it. Whatsoever, therefore, we see, is only a compound. Further, we find that all visible and tangible objects are reducible to such a fine state that physical division of them at length becomes impracticable; and that, when these invisible fine particles unite again with one another, they can again form visible and tangible objects. Consequently, the first conclusion at which we arrive from the above method is, that of the Naiyâyakas (Indian School of Logic), who think that the matter, of which the world is formed, consists of atoms or extremely small particles which are incapable of further division and which are besides indestructible in their nature. Holding this theory for the present, we must conclude that whatever exists in the world, being but a compound of atoms, there must have been a time when the components of the compound, namely the atoms themselves. existed separately. In other words, there must have been a time when the world did not exist in its present visible condition. Besides we must also expect a time when this compound will resolve again into its original components. When atoms unite together, and form Compounds, the process is the Evolution of the World, and when

* For a fuller account of the process of the composition of the elements and their product—the material universe—, one must study S'ri S'ankarâchârya's Panchi Karana.

they disintegrate, it is Dissolution, or, more properly, Involution. The final result, based on this atomic theory is, that a series of Evolutions and Involutions is stretched out ad-infinitum.

But on further consideration, it will be found that the result arrived at is not free from objections. To a student of atomic theory, doubts will arise as to the correctness of the doctrine of the indivisibility, of atoms. He will think that a thing, in order to be indivisible, must be without dimensions. He will go on to argue that an atom cannot be conceived as one without dimensions for according to him a combination of atoms produces an object having dimensions, and is, therefore, divisible. He will thus come to the conclusion, and rightly so, that so long as it can be asserted that a combination of atoms can form an object with the dimensions, it might be safely argued that an atom can be divided ad-infinitum mentally, though not physically. It will appear to him that an atom cannot, in fact, be the ultimate unit of matter as the Atomists believe : he thus detects the error in the atomic theory, and finds it untenable.

After this, the conclusions arrived at by the Sânkhya system will commend themselves better to him. The author of this system considers with the Atomist, the visible matter to be a real entity ; but he does not hold that the material world is composed of atoms ; he rather believes that the cause of the visible objects is an indiscernable principle, which he calls by the name of Prakriti. This, according to him, was originally an aggregate of three qualities, *viz.*, Satwaguna (Lightness or Goodness), Rajaguna (Activity), and Tamaguna (Inertia) in an equipoise state. He thinks that this Prakriti, the primordial matter when modified became manifest in the form of the visible world, which he calls Vikriti—that is, the world as it now exists. According to his views there was a time when the world did not exist in its present visible state, and consequently there will come a time when it will cease to exist in its present form. According to him when the Prakriti undergoes a change, and consequent manifestations take place, it is called Evolution, and when the manifestations revert to the original condition, it is called Involution ; he thinks, moreover, that these Evolutions and Involutions go on ad-infinitum. We need not here discuss the arguments by which the Vedântic system of Philosophy refutes the Sânkhya theory, and proves that the phenomenal world is but a great illusion.

The theory that Evolutions and Involutions take place ad-infinitum is, however, supported by the Vedas and Simritis.*

The views of Mr. Herbert Spencer, the great English thinker of the presest day, in regard to the theory of Evolution and Involution, correspond with those of the author of the Sânkhya system of Philosophy. At the end of his Chapter on Dissolution (First Principles) he says :—

Para. 183. "Thus we are led to the conclusion that the entire process of things, as displayed in the aggregate of the visible universe, is analogous to the entire process of things as displayed in the smallest aggregates."

"Motion as well as matter being fixed in quantity, it would seem that the change in the distribution of matter which motion effects, coming to a limit in whichever direction it is carried, the indestructible motion thereupon necessitates a reverse distribution. Apparently, the universally co-existent forces of attraction and repulsion, which, as we have seen, necessitate rhythm in all minor changes throughout the Universe, also necessitate rhythm in the totality of its changes—produce now an immeasurable period during which the attractive forces predominating, cause universal concentration, and then an immeasurable period during which the repulsive forces predominating, cause universal diffusion—alternate eras of Evolution and Dissolution. And thus there

* *Vide* the Rig-Veda Mantra quoted in the beginning of Chapter I, and Manu Smriti, Chapter I, S'loke 80, quoted at the end of Chapter I, Part I. of this book.

is suggested the conception of a past during which there have been successive Evolutions analogous to that which is now going on; and a future during which successive other such Evolutions may go on ever the same in principal but never the same in concrete result."

Christians and Mohamedans also believe that the present universe was created at one time, and will ultimately dissolve.

We have tried to demonstrate, in Chapter I, Part I, of this work, that the theory of Evolution and Involution, as understood by us, is the only one which can stand the test of reason and science.

II. Re-incarnation of the Conscious Soul (Jivâtmâ).

It will not be out of place here to reinforce our argument regarding the theory of re-incarnation, as propounded in Chapter II of this work.

If all human beings were equally endowed with physical and mental gifts, and equally placed in social life, or, in other words, if there were no inequality amongst them, but which is present in everything around us, no question could arise as to any previous existence or past actions of individual souls. But when, on the contrary, we find that no two things are exactly alike, and that whichever side we glance we find diversity, there naturally arises the question—how and why all this difference?

The followers of Christ and Mohammad believe that the present embodied existence of the individual souls is their first incarnation, and that for the acts of this short life, where God has so pleased to place them in unequal circumstances, they will be eternally punished or rewarded at the day of Judgment; and thus they are at a loss to reconcile God's Justice with His mercy. While both these religions preach the principle "As we sow, so we reap," it is difficult to understand why the same rule is not applied by them to the circumstances of our present life, as the result of our acts in our past life or lives.

I have tried to prove this doctrine in Part I, Chapter II, on scientific grounds, with examples of every-day occurrence.

I find that the doctrine of crucifixion of Christ and his resurrection from the grave is, in other words the doctrine of Re-incarnation of Souls. Accordingly, Paul, the Apostle, who is a commentator on Christ's preachings, clearly explains this doctrine in Chapter XV of his First Epistle to the Corinthians. He says :—

12. "Now if Christ be preached that he rose from the dead, how say some among you that there is no resurrection of the dead ?"

13. "But if there be no resurrection of the dead, then is Christ not risen."

14. "And if Christ be not risen, then *is* our preaching vain, and your faith *is* also vain."

15. "Yea, and we are found false witnesses of God; because we have testified of God that he raised up Christ: whom he raised not up, if so be that the dead rise not."

16. "For if the dead rise not, then is not Christ raised :"

. . . .

32. "If after the manner of men I have fought with beasts at Ephesus, what advantageth it me, if the dead rise not? Let us eat and drink; for to-morrow we die."

33. "Be not deceived: evil communications corrupt good manners."

34. "Awake to righteousness, and sin not; for some have not the knowledge of God: I speak *this* to your shame."

35. "But some *man* will say, How are the dead raised up? and with what body do they come ?"

36. "*Thou* fool, that which thou sowest is not quickened, except it die :"

37. "And that which thou sowest, thou sowest not that body that shall be, but bare grain, it may chance of wheat, or of some other *grain* :

38. "But God giveth it a body as it hath pleased him, and to every seed his own body."

39. "All flesh *is* not the same flesh : but *there is* one *kind of* flesh of men, another flesh of beasts, another of fishes, *and* another of birds."

40. "*There are* also celestial bodies, and bodies terrestrial: but the glory of the celestial *is* one and the *glory* of the terrestrial *is* another."

41. "There *is* one glory of the sun, and another glory of the moon, and another glory of the stars: for *one* star differeth from *another* star in glory."

42. "So also *is* the resurrection of the dead. It is sown in corruption; it is raised in incorruption:"

43. "It is sown in dishonour; it is raised in glory: it is sown in weakness; it is raised in power:"

44. "It is sown a natural body; it is raised a spiritual body." . . . .
. . . .

51. "Behold, I shew you a mystery; we shall not at all sleep, but we shall all be changed."

The reader will notice here that Paul makes no distinction between the rising of the Lord Jesus and that of other persons after death; and he shows in the example of the seed, that the dead do not rise with the same body they had when they were buried, but with another body as it may please God.

Mr. Herbert Spencer, speaking of conduct as the cause of good and bad consequences, says*:—

32. "During every phase of civilization, the actions of the Unseen Reality, as well as the resulting rewards and punishments, being conceivable only in such form as experience furnishes, to supplant them by higher ones before wider experiences have made higher ones conceivable, is to set up vague and uninfluential motives for definite and influential

* First Principles, Part I, 4th Edition.

ones. Even now, for the great mass of men, unable through lack of culture to trace out with due clearness those good and bad consequences which conduct brings round through the established order of the Unknowable, it is needful that there should be vividly depicted future torments and future joys—pains and pleasures of a definite kind, produced in a manner direct and simple enough to be clearly imagined. Nay still more must be conceded. Few if any are as yet fitted wholly to dispense with such conceptions as are current. The highest abstractions take so great a mental power to realize with any vividness, and are so inoperative upon conduct unless they are vividly realized, that their regulative effects must for a long period to come be appreciable on but a small minority. To see clearly how a right or wrong act generates consequences, internal and external, that go on branching out more widely as years progress, requires a rare power of analysis. To mentally represent even a single series of those consequences, as it stretches out into the remote future, requires an equally rare power of imagination. And to estimate these consequences in their totality, ever multiplying in number while diminishing in intensity, requires a grasp of thought possessed by none. Yet it is only by such analysis, such imagination, and such grasp, that conduct can be rightly guided in the absence of all other control: only so can ultimate rewards and penalties be made to outweigh proximate pains and pleasures, Indeed, were it not that throughout the progress of the race, man's experiences of the effects of conduct have been slowly generalized into principles—were it not that these principles have been from generation to generation insisted on by parents, upheld by public opinion, sanctified by religion, and enforced by threats of eternal damnation for disobedience—were it not that under these potent influences, habits have been modified, and the feelings proper to them made innate—were it not, in short, that we have been rendered in a considerable degree organically moral; it is certain that disastrous results would ensue from the removal of those strong and distinct motives which the current belief supplies. Even as it is, those who relinquish the faith in which they have been brought up, for *this most abstract faith in which science and religion unite*,* may not uncommonly fail to act up to their convictions. Left to their organic morality, enforced only by general reasonings imperfectly wrought out and difficult to keep before the mind, their defects of nature will often come out more strongly than they would have done under their previous creed. The substituted creed can become adequately operative only when it becomes, like the present one, an element in early education, and has the support of a strong social sanction. Nor will men be quite ready for it until, through the continuance of a discipline which has already partially moulded them to the conditions of social existence, they are completely moulded to those conditions."

The belief in the immortality of the soul, and its re-incarnation, as a consequence of the good or bad actions (Karma) performed by men in their former lives, constitutes the grand and vast platform, on which men of all creeds and races may meet if they rightly understand the esoteric meaning of their exoteric church religion. All persons should know that every one of them will be judged by his own acts, and no mediator will be allowed to intervene between *him* and the effects of his deeds. Jesus Christ has expressed this principle of Divine Justice in a very clear and concise manner in Mathew, Chapter VII, Verses 21 to 23.

21. "Not every one that saith unto me, Lord, Lord, shall enter into the kingdom of Heaven; but he that doth the will of my Father which is in Heaven."

22. "Many will say to me in that day, Lord, Lord, have we not prophesied in thy name? and in thy name have cast out devils? and in thy name done many wonderful works?"

23. "And then will I profess unto them, I never knew you: depart from me, ye that work iniquity."

As already noted, I have explained in Chapter II, Part I, of this work, how the human soul is considered responsible

---

* The italics are mine.

for its actions and has to experience their result by undergoing re-incarnation, and now the actions of the present life become the seed for the next incarnation, which may raise us to the status of gods inhabiting the sun, moon and the stars, or degrade us to the level of the lower animals or of insects, herbs or stones. As it is with the individual man so it is with the universe. The aggregate result of all the different actions of the previous Kalpa has become the cause of the present cycle (Kalpa), and the actions of the present cycle will, in their turn, become the seed of the next future Evolution, and so on *ad infinitum*.

III. Human origin and the Vedic Revelation.

Our Vedic theory of Evolution and Involution differs from the untenable theory of Naturalists. The latter believe in "the survival of the fittest." But if this belief be accepted, there would really be no dissolution of the universe, because then a continual improvement and consequently a change for the better will go on for ever ; and thus there will never be a dissolution or an end of the present manifestation. When they admit that an Evolution is going on, or in other words, that there is a beginning of the manifestation of the phenomenal world, it is strange that, having believed in one end of the thread, they do not believe in Involution, which is the other end of the manifestation. According to the Vedic theory the best days of the world are the earlier ones. In course of time development is completed, the energies are weakened, till at length the manifested nature is exhausted and no longer possesses any productive power ; and consequently requires rest to recoup its lost strength (*vide* Chapter I, Part I).

The Vedic theory is also supported by tradition and ancient books, which tell us that the people of previous ages were more robust and strong, and enjoyed longer leases of life than the people of the present day.

The theory of natural selection is indicative of nature's imperfections. According to it Nature is still improving. This theory points out the absence in Nature at present of the best forms that it will produce in the future. We on the other hand, believe in the pre-existence of all things in Nature, and in their later manifestation, not as original things but the various forms as manifestation of a pre-existing substance, lying latent in its bosom Our doctrine is, that nothing can come out of nothing. Therefore, whatever comes in existence, must have had a pre-existence in Nature. We have thus little respect for a theory such as that of Darwin which propounds that human species are a development of an inferior animal nature. For, if we were to accept this, we would be at a loss to trace the origin of human language and the possession of Divine knowledge, which are peculiar to mankind only, and which (*vide* Chapter III, Part I) are not self-acquired, but can only be learnt from others. Such theories may perhaps find supporters among those races which were originally savage, and which had improved within the memory of man. For, such races are apt to think that as their present development from a savage to a civilized state is a well-known fact, it may be possible that man himself is a development of the ape like species. But the hypothesis which makes this theory possible is not reasonable in itself. No savage nation has ever become self-civilized; and we can always trace the civilization of one nation to another which is already civilized. The thoughts of learned men which pass as original, can be traced to the authors whom they have studied, or to the society in which they have lived and moved. With us, the Aryans of India, it is quite different. We have the very word of him (Manu), who was the founder of the human race, telling us that mankind is from the beginning a separate species of the animal kingdom, and that the highest thoughts within the reach of mankind were revealed to him; and he, in his turn, revealed the same to his descendents. The knowledge of Self or Divine Essence, is the highest truth worth realizing, and this truth was explained by Brahmâ (the first Manu), in the beginning of the world to his eldest son Atharva, The word revealed to this Brahmâ is the Holy Veda, and the latter is, therefore, in itself an authority as to its being divine and superhuman.

The Veda does not repeat the historical facts which men with common intelligence can write, but it explains the higher truths which man, with his common sense and intellect, is not able to do. It treats of the immortality of the soul, Jivātmâ, its re-incarnation, the way that leads to the knowledge of Self, and finally the mode of acquiring that knowledge which removes ignorance and secures emancipation from individuality; when the soul finds itself as the one All pervading Entity Such knowledge cannot be self-acquired, but becomes comprehensible only by revelation from the proper source: So says Manu in Chapter XII, S'lokas 95 to 97.

IV. Teachings of the Veda.

95. " Such codes of law as are not grounded on the Veda; and the various heterodox theories of men, produce no good fruit after death; for they all are declared to have their origin in darkness."

96. " All systems which are repugnant to the Veda, must have been composed by mortals, and shall soon perish; their modern date proves them vain and false."

97. " The three words, the four classes of men and their four distinct orders, with all that has been, all that is, and all that will be, are made known by the Veda."

Chapter V, which treats of the Removal of Sin, is clear enough, and does not require any explanation here.

Chapter VI, deals with the subject of Upâsnâ or meditation, as a step towards the attainment of Divine knowledge. In it I have explained the philosophy of symbolic worship or Pratika Upâsnâ which is now often termed by the contemptuous name of 'Idol Worship.'

Removal of Vikshepa (Unsteadiness of Mind).

All philosophers agree on the point that whatever is an object of conception or perception is finite, and hence liable to change. But the common belief is, that God is Absolute.

Infinite and Unchangeable. God is not, therefore, an object of conception or perception and He cannot really be worshipped mentally or physically. The natural result of this would be agnosticism and the abandonment of all worship; and, in course of time, total ignorance about the Divine Principle. It is probably for reasons like this that the Vedas teach symbolic worship of the Deity, which can neither be comprehended by the mind nor cognised at all by the senses.

The word meditation, as defined by Mr. Coleridge,* is equivalent to the Sanskrit word Dhyâna, which is really a function of the memory, namely, to bring to mind what has been already known. The Sanskrit word Adhyâsa means attributing the nature of one thing to another. This is of two kinds. One is called *Sambâdi* or beneficial, and the other is called *Bisambâdi* or injurious. The former is a wilful act of the mind, and the latter is, as it were, forced on the mind. It is a Bisambâdi Adhyâsa, when a rope appears to be a serpent, or as in a mirage when a sandy desert appears as a lake with fertile surroundings, without any will on our part; and this is injurious. It is a Sambâdi Adhyâsa when we, by an act of our mind, contemplate a thing to be what it really is not. For instance, we draw certain features on a piece of paper, and we call it a picture of a friend. We look at it, and feel a satisfaction in it. This satisfaction, being the result of a wilful act of the mind, is beneficial. The picture, in this instance, is only a symbol representing our friend. So are the photos, busts, remembrances and so forth, symbols of the objects they bring to memory. The realization of God's existence is His knowledge or Jnâna, and His contemplation by symbols is the symbolic worship or Pratika Upâsnâ. The latter is always performed in absence of the real object of worship, and this mode of worship proves beneficial in two ways, *viz.*, (1) that the worshipper

---

* For *meditation* is, I presume, that act of the mind by which it seeks within, either the law of the phenomena which it has contemplated without, or semblances, symbols, and analogies corresponsive to the same.

Webster.

by meditating on a symbol acquires the habit of concentrating his mind on one object; and (2) that a keen desire arises in the mind of the meditator to know the Reality whose symbol is the object of his meditation and worship.

This theory of symbolic adoration appears to be at the bottom of animal sacrifice and other modes of religious worship. Evidently the Jews believed in the efficacy of animal and human sacrifice in purifying a man from sinfulness and securing divine pleasure. It appears that, following the above principle of symbolic worship, the God of Abraham permitted him (Abraham) to kill a ram in place of his son Isac. Jesus Christ also taught this principle of symbolic worship to his disciples, as shown in the Gospel of Mathew, Chapter XXVI, in the following words :—

26. "And as they were eating, Jesus took bread, and blessed *it*, and brake *it*, and gave *it* to the disciples, and said, Take, eat; this is my body."

27. "And he took the cup, and gave thanks, and gave *it* to them, saying, Drink ye all of it;"

28. "For this is my blood of the New Testament, which is shed for many for the remission of sins."

It is clear from the above that Jesus Christ meant to teach his disciples a method of worship by symbols, and it is by virtue of this worship, that the Christians, in celebrating the Commission, still believe that the bread they eat is symbolic of the body, and the wine they drink symbolic of the blood of Christ. When the reverend missionaries themselves thus believe in symbolic worship, they ought not to view with disdain, the symbol-worshipping Hindus who do not believe the images they set up to be any thing but mere symbols.

Mohammedans too are not free from symbolic worship. They say that God is *Lá Makân* (having no particular place of residence), yet they worship *Kaaba*, believing it to be *Beit Allâh* (House of God). It is on account of this belief, that a Musalmân dares not sleep with his feet towards the Kaaba;

and that in order that his prayers be of any benefit to him, he must recite them with his face towards the house of God in Mecca.

Thus it appears that the founders of those religons which professed to teach that all forms of symbol worship should be severely reprobated, have, in spite of their teachings, found themselves unable to avoid symbol worship under all circumstances. Truly speaking all worship, other than symbolic, must have as its object an ideal existing in the mind of the worshipper. Does not a Mohammedan think it a religious act to repeat the name of God? I would ask what the 'Name' itself is. Is it not a symbol of the Unknown? Are not the names of persons and things the symbols to denote those persons and things? The worship of an idol, which he sets up as the symbol of God, brings to the worshipper the satisfaction of worshipping a visible something which is within his comprehension and has apparently substantial existence; while he who worships God as a creation of his mind, without the help of an internal or external symbol, is the worshipper of an idea, which constantly changes, and, as compared with an external symbol, has a much less permanent existence.

The above remarks apply also to those newly-founded religious sects, who have contracted the contagion of hatred for symbolic worship from their Christian and Mohammedan neighbours. It would be a blasphemy on their part to call God Father (Pitâ) or Mother (Mâ â) unless the words Father and Mother are used in symbolical sense, and their otherwise Unknowable God is thus symbolized; whereas, if these words represent no ideals, then their pathetic addresses are useless. If their God is a God *with qualities*, He is then certainly liable to change and is finite; and, therefore, cannot be Absolute. But if He is, as they believe Him to be, an Absolute, Infinite, Unchangeable God, He can neither be imagined nor described, and, therefore, He is in fact one that cannot be directly worshipped. It may, therefore, be said that unless these people will learn the philosophy of symbolic worship, all their prayers and worship will end in nothing, because He, to whom they pray in qualifying terms, is not such as they think Him to be.

VII. Aum as the Symbol of God.

This being so, it becomes necessary to use symbols for that which cannot be represented by words or by ideas, and which is Indescribable and Undefinable. As given in Dr. Webster's dictionary, Mr. Coleridge defines the word 'Symbol' as follows :—

"A symbol is a sign included in the idea which it represents, *e. g.* an actual part chosen to represent the whole or a lower form or species used as the representative of a higher in the same kind."

In selecting symbols, it is always the rule that one lower is designed to signify one higher, for it is elevating to do so. The Vedas, therefore, lay down that the sacred monosyllable 'Aum' (ओम्) is a symbol of the Absolute Deity. Chapters VIII, IX and X of Part I, and the whole of Part II, treat fully of the points in which the symbol and the original are analogous and similar.

XI. Evidence from sounds in Nature of the Symbol Aum.

In Chapter XI, we have shown that the sounds produced by certain animals have a resemblance to the pronunciation of the syllable 'Aum' or 'Aung,' and though some may at first sight laugh at the examples given there, they will when they begin to appreciate the philosophy propounded, be better able to judge and value them. The philosophy on which this theory is founded, has been fully explained in Chapter VII, by showing that it is the vowels only that have a sound of their own, and that all the elementary vowels are contained in the monosyllabe Aum, which may, therefore, be properly called the whole speech or the compendium of speech. This being a fact, articulations and sounds must either be the ennunciation of the full syllable or a part of it, whether in a correct form or otherwise

---

At the end of Chapter XI, I have given illustrations, showing that the triliteral monosyllable Aum and the Âtmâ of which it is a symbol, have manifested themselves into trinities, in the formation of Speech and the Universe respectively. To avoid misapprehension as to the origin of the Doctrine of Trinity, it appears necessary here to say a few words.

The Doctrine of Christian Trinity explained.

The Vedas treat of the Doctrine of Trinity and it is still believed by the professors of the Vedic religion. This doctrine appears to have travelled on from India to Egypt, Greece and other places.

Jesus Christ, though born in Bethlehem in Judea, was nourished and brought up in Egypt.* He, therefore, apparently received his spiritual education in Egypt. Saint Paul calls him a High Priest after the order of Melchisedec.† Having returned from Egypt, Jesus Christ preached to his disciples and the people of Judea, the Doctrine of Unity in Trinity and Trinity in Unity. This doctrine appears to have been understood, to some extent, by his followers‡; but from time immemorial it has apparently remained a mystery.

The Christians of the present day are really at a loss to account for their strange doctrine of *Three in One and One in Three*; and this doctrine, it may be said, will ever remain unintelligible to them, until they will kneel at the feet of the Vedic philosophers and learn from them the mystery about 'The Fourth,' which is the real Entity and of which the others are mere manifestations. If we keep in view 'The Fourth,' the Doctrine of Trinity is easily comprehended. The three personages of the Christian Trinity are the manifestations of the One (Real Entity), and the One (Entity) is manifested in the Three. If on the other hand, we believe that the three personages of the Trinity viz., the Father, Son and the Holy Ghost, are three

* S. Mathew's Gospel Chapter II, Verses 3 to 15 and 19 to 21.

† Paul's Epistle to the Hebrews, Chapter VI, Verse 20 and Chapter VII, Verses 17 and 21.

‡ Paul's First Epistle to the Corinthians, Chapter XIII, Verses 9-13.

separate Entities, then Three cannot be One and One cannot be Three. If any one would say that the Three Entities unite together to form One, then this *One*, a compound of the Three, will be a *Fourth*, different from each of the other Three. The very thought of Three in One and One in Three is impossible without the existence of a Fourth, and if there be no Fourth, the only combination that can be formed out of Three, will be Two in One and One in Two.

The Vedic followers believe in the three-fold manifestations of One God, respectively known as Brahmâ the Creator, Vishnu the Protector, and Shiva the Destroyer. In other words, he is described as Virâta or Vaishvanara (Gross Manifestation of the Universe), Hiranyagarbha (Subtle Manifestation of the Universe) and I'shwara (Unmanifested Universe). The 'Fourth,' of which all the Three are manifestations, is called in Sanskrit Âtmâ (the All pervading).

As Atmâ always appears to us in Three Manifestations, the ancients regarded the numeral three as a sacred number. In order to worship this Âtmâ together with its three conditions, the Vedic followers made a symbol of it. This symbol, they represented by the figure 卐 or more briefly + and gave it the name of Ganesh or the Lord of all Deities. On all sacred and ceremonial occasions, this figure was invariably drawn out, and worshipped as the foremost deity, being always assigned the first place among the Gods in the order of their worship. This is done by the Vedic followers even up to the present day. This mark represents four parts, three of them resting on the Fourth and the Fourth supporting the other three. This symbol also appears to have been adopted by the Christians as signifying the Cross on which Jesus Christ was crucified. It is not really a mark of the Cross, but a symbol of the Three Manifestations of the Divine Entity. The figure itself is a solution of the difficult problem of Trinity, and although every Christian recognises this symbol, but being ignorant of the Fourth is unable to understand the doctrine of Trinity which he believes through faith alone.

Chapters XIII and XIV are clear enough and need no comment here. It is likely that the orthodox Mohammedans will not approve of the explanation of the letters Alif, Lâm, and Mim as given by me, though they have not as yet given any satisfactory explanation themselves. To say that they are merely meaningless letters, would evidently call into question the genuineness of the divine source of Al-Korân.

Traces of 'Aum' in the Koran and the old Testament.

I would, therefore, like to draw the attention of the unprejudiced Mohammedan reader to the first verse of the Second Chapter of the Korân, which begins with the words "*Alif, Lâm Mim*; this is the book, there is no doubt in it" . . . . Now the word 'this' refers to the letters preceding it, and means that these three letters are the whole book. The word 'this' cannot, as some would interpret, mean the whole volume of the Korân as it is extant now-a-days; because, when the above-noted verse was repeated by the Prophet, the Korân was not received in full: it was received in parts over the course of several years. The majority of the Mohammedans would feel contented with the explanation that these letters are a mystery, and with them all efforts to find a solution are useless.

A truth is after all a truth. We have shown how *Alif, Lâm and Mim* (A, L & M) of the Korân are the same letters अ (A), उ (U) and म् (M) of ओम् (Aum). I have also tried in Chapter XIV to trace these letters in the Old Testament.

In Chapter XV, with which the first part ends are given some extracts from Hindu religious books to show the sanctity of these letters.

Part II consists of the text of the Sanskrit Mândúkya Upanishad of the Atharva Veda, with an English translation of it, and a full commentary on the same, following in the lines of S'ri Gaurapâda Âchârya and S'ri S'ankara Âchârya.

The Mândúkya Upanishad of the Atharva Veda.

The first S'ruti states that the word 'Aum' is a symbol as

well as the name of the Universal soul, and that all that is Manifest and Unmanifest is one and the same Divine Entity. The second S'ruti says that this Aumkâra is also called Brahma and Âtmâ, and is known as having four feet, or, more properly speaking, conditions. The third, fourth and fifth S'rutis show that the first, second and third conditions of this Âtmâ, are the wakeful, dreamy and dreamless (slumbering) states respectively. The sixth S'ruti sings the praise of the third condition, and explains the powers which are displayed by Âtmâ while it appears in this condition. The seventh S'ruti states that the Fourth is not a condition like the preceding three but that it is the Entity itself, which appears to us in three separate aspects, that in itself it is free of all conditions. and that this Âtmâ which is 'the self of all,' should be known. It is to be inferred from this S'ruti that Âtmâ is knowable. The eighth S'ruti explains that, as the full syllable Aum is a symbol of Âtmâ, each of its letters is a symbol of each of the three conditions of Âtmâ in their respective order. S'rutis nine, ten and eleven respectively show that the letter 'A' of the syllable Aum, is a symbol of the Virâta phase (Gross Manifestation), 'U' of the Hiranyagarbha (Subtle Manifestation) and 'M' of the I'shwara phase (Unmanifested state) of Âtmâ. These S'rutis also give the analogies between symbols and their originals, as well as the benefits which the meditator reaps by meditating on each phase. S'ruti twelve, with which the Upanishad ends, tells us what is meant by 'The Fourth' and the way how one who knows 'The Fourth' attains emancipation.

S'rutis 7 and 12 indicate by mere allusion what Âtmâ is: the former enjoins that it (Âtmâ) should be known; and the latter says that he that knows this Âtmâ, is emancipated. Here arises a seeming conflict. How can that which is not an object of conception or perception, become an object of knowledge (conception)? Though Mr. Herbert Spencer has arrived at a correct and sound conclusion* that there is only

* First Principles Part I, 4th Edition.

one Absolute Non-Relative Entity; yet, being ignorant of the method by which the knowledge of this Entity is acquired, he was unable to realize it; and it is a matter of great regret that he dogmatized this Entity as "Unknowable." Consequently, the Agnostics think it a waste of energy to make any effort to seek for a solution. The following quotations from Mr. Herbert Spencer's First Principles will show the views held by him regarding the relative world and the Non-Relative Absolute Entity :—

Ultimate Religious Ideas. Chapter II page 46, last para.

1. "Here, then, is an ultimate religious truth of the highest possible certainty—a truth in which religions in general are at one with each other, and with a philosophy antagonistic to their special dogmas. And this truth, respecting which there is a latent agreement among all mankind from the fetish-worshipper to the most stoical critic of human creeds, must be the one we seek. If Religion and Science are to be reconciled, the basis of reconciliation must be this deepest, widest, and most certain of all facts—that the Power which the Universe manifests to us is utterly inscrutable."

Space and Time. Chapter III, pege 50.

2. "It results therefore that Space and Time are wholly incomprehensible. The immediate knowledge which we seem to have of them, proves, when examined, to be total ignorance. While our belief in their objective reality is insurmountable, we are unable to give any rational account of it. And to posit the alternative belief (possible to state but impossible to realize) merely to multiply irrationalities."

Matter, page 54.

3. "Matter then, in its ultimate nature, is as absolutely incomprehensible as Space and Time. Frame what suppositions we may, we find on tracing out their implications that they leave us nothing but a choice between opposite absurdities."

4. "Thus neither when considered in connection with Space, nor when considered in connection with Matter, nor when considered in connection with Rest, do we find that Motion is truly cognizable. All efforts to understand its essential nature do but bring us to alternative impossibilities of thought."

Motion page 58.

5. "While, then, it is impossible to form any idea of Force in itself, it is equally impossible to comprehend its mode of exercise."

Force page 61.

6. "As we found it was impossible really to conceive Rest becoming Motion or Motion becoming Rest; so here we find it is impossible really to conceive either the beginning or the ending of those changes which constitute Consciousness."

Consciousness, page 63.

"Hence, while we are unable either to believe or to conceive that the duration of Consciousness is infinite, we are equally unable either to know it as finite, or to conceive it as finite."

7. "Passing over this, however, it may readily be shown that a cognition of self, properly so called, is absolutely negatived by the law of thought. The fundamental condition to all consciousness, emphatically insisted upon by Mr. Mansel in common with Sir William Hamilton and others, is the antithesis of subject and object. And on this "primitive dualism of consciousness, from which the explanations of philosophy must take their start," Mr. Mansel founds his refutation of the German Absolutists. But now, what is the corollary from this doctrine, as bearing on the consciousness of self? The mental act in which self is known, implies, like every other mental act, a perceiving subject and a perceived object. If, then, the object perceived is self, what is the subject that perceives? or if it is the true self which thinks, what other self can it be that is thought of? Clearly, a true cognition of self implies a state in which the knower and the known are one—in which subject and object are

Cognition of self, pages 65 and 66.

identified ; and this Mr. Mansel rightly holds to be the annihilation of both."

"So that the personality of which each is conscious, and of which the existence is to each a fact beyond all others the most certain, is yet a thing which cannot truly be known at all; knowledge of it is forbidden by the very nature of thought."

Ultimate scientific ideas, pp. 66 and 67.

8. "Objective and subjective things he thus ascertains to be alike inscrutable in their substance and genesis. In all directions his investigations eventually bring him face to face with an insoluble enigma; and he ever more clearly perceives it to be an insoluble enigma. He learns at once the greatness and the littleness of the human intellect—its power in dealing with all that comes within the range of experience; its impotence in dealing with all that transcends experience. He realizes with a special vividness the utter incomprehensibleness of the simplest fact, considered in itself. He, more than any other, truly *knows* that in its ultimate essence nothing can be known."

Unthinkableness of the Unconditioned, page 82.

9. "Thus, from the very nature of thought, the relativity of our knowledge is inferable in three several ways. As we find by analysing it, and as we see it objectively displayed in every proposition, a thought involves *relation, difference, likeness.* Whatever does not present each of these does not admit of cognition. And hence we may say that the unconditioned, as presenting none of them, is trebly Unthinkable."

An indefinite consciousness of the Absolute, pp. 88 and 89.

10. "Observe in the first place, that every one of the arguments by which the relativity of our knowledge is demonstrated, distinctly postulates the positive existence of something beyond the relative. To say that we cannot know the Absolute, is, by implication, to affirm that there *is* an Absolute. In the very denial of our power to learn *what* the Absolute is, there lies hidden the assumption *that* it is; and the making

of this assumption proves that the Absolute has been present to the mind, not as a nothing, but as a something. Similarly with every step in the reasoning by which this doctrine is upheld. The Noumenon, everywhere named as the antithesis of the phenomenon, is throughout necessarily thought of as an actuality. It is rigorously impossible to conceive that our knowledge is a *knowledge of Appearances only, without at the same time conceiving a Reality of which they are appearances*;* for appearance without reality is unthinkable. Strike out from the argument the terms Unconditioned, Infinite, Absolute, with their equivalents, and in place of them write, "Negation of conceivability," or "absence of the conditions under which consciousness is possible," and you find that the argument becomes nonsense. Truly to realize in thought any one of the propositions of which the argument consists, the Unconditioned must be represented as positive and not negative. How then can it be a legitimate conclusion from the argument, that our consciousness of it is negative? An argument, the very construction of which assigns 'to a certain term a certain meaning, but which ends in showing that this term has no such meaning, is simply an elaborate suicide. Clearly, then, the very demonstration that a *definite* consciousness of the Absolule is impossible to us, unavoidably presupposes an *indefinite* consciousness of it."

Distinction between Relative and Non-Relative, pages 95 and 96.

II. "The distinction we feel between special and general existence, is the distinction between that which is changeable in us and that which is unchangeable. The contrast between the Absolute and the Relative in our minds is really the contrast between that mental element which exists Absolutely, and those which exist relatively."

. . . .

"To sum up this somewhat too elaborate argument:—We have seen how in the very assertion that all our knowledge, properly so called, is Relative, there is involved the assertion

---

* The italics in this sentence are mine.

that there exists a Non-relative. We have seen how, in each step of the argument by which this doctrine is established, the same assumption is made. We have seen how, from the very necessity of thinking in relations, it follows that the Relative is itself inconceivable, except as related to a real Non-relative. We have seen that unless a real Non-relative or Absolute be postulated, the Relative itself becomes Absolute; and so brings the Argument to a contradiction. And on contemplating the process of thought, we have equally seen how impossible it is to get rid of the consciousness of an actuality lying behind appearances; and how, from this impossibility, results our indestructible belief in that actuality."

Inability to know the Absolute Reality, page 110.

(12) "In all imaginable ways we find thrust upon us the truth, that we are not permitted to know—nay are not even permitted to conceive—that Reality which is behind the veil of Appearance; and yet it is said to be our duty to believe (and in so far to conceive) that this Reality exists in a certain defined manner. Shall we call this reverence? or shall we call it the reverse?"

"Volumes might be written upon the impiety of the pious."

Inability to know the Unconditioned, page 113.

(13) "By continually seeking to know and being continually thrown back with a deepened conviction of the impossibility of knowing, we may keep alive the consciousness that it is alike our highest wisdom and our highest duty to regard that through which all things exist as the Unknowable."

Postulates, page 157.

(14) "In brief, our postulates are:—an Unknowable Power; the existence of Knowable likenesses and differences among the manifestations of that Power; and a resulting segregation of the manifestations into those of subject and object."

(15) "Hence there may be drawn these conclusions:—

Conclusions, page 161.

First, that we have an indefinite consciousness of an Absolute Reality transcending relations, which is produced by the absolute persistence in us of something which servives all changes of relation. Second, that we have a definite consciousness of Relative Reality, which unceasingly persists in us under one or other of its forms, and under each form so long as the conditions of presentation are fulfilled; and that the Relative Reality, being thus continuously presistent in us, is as real to us as would be the Absolute Reality could it be immediately known. Third, that thought being possible only under relation, the Relative Reality can be conceived as such only in connexion with an Absolute Reality; and the connexion between the two being absolutely persistent in our consciousness, is real in the same sense as the terms it unites are real."

Comparison of Mr. Spencer's Views with the Vedânta Philosophy.

From these quotations, the reader will find, that Mr. Herbert Spencer agrees with the Vedântists in holding that there is only one Reality underlying all phenomena; and *that all the phenomena being only Appearances are true only in their relative nature*; but he differs in thinking that the Real Entity is Unknowable in its Ultimate Non-relative nature.

The Reality underlying all phenomena, is called in Sanskrit Âtmâ (the all-pervading self-same Spirit), and the Phenomena, which though relatively true have no absolute real existence of their own, and depend for their very appearance on the Real Entity, are known as Nâma and Rupa (Nâma means 'name,' and Rupa literally meaning 'form' is indicative of all the five perceptions), and are stated to be illusive in their nature. The reason why this phenomenal world is called Illusive, and sometimes Anirvachniya (one about which nothing can be said definitely) is, that it appears relatively true, but when searched in its ultimate nature, no signs of its substance can be traced. It can, therefore, be neither stated as true nor untrue. It is different both from Existence and Non-existence. It has thus a mere relative existence but no existence in its ultimate nature. Mr. Herbert Spencer agrees with this statement when he says*—" It is rigorously impossible to conceive that our knowledge is a knowledge of appearances only, without at the same time conceiving a Reality of which they are appearances; for appearances without reality are unthinkable." By this he evidently means that the Relative World is only a manifestation of the Real Power and not a Reality in itself.

As regards Âtmâ (the Reality), which according to Mr. Herbert Spencer is Unknowable, the Vedântists affirm that Its existence is realized in the act of comprehending the different ideas arising in the mind.

Different modes of proof.

Before criticizing the views of Mr. Herbert Spencer relating to the unknowableness of Âtmâ, we would first describe the different modes and methods by which knowledge of things both objective and subjective is acquired.

The manifestation in the form of mind and the senses is called Pramâna Chaitanya or Instrument of Cognition. The Âtmâ, in conjunction with the mind and the senses, is called Pramâtâ Chaitanya, or the Cognizor. And the phenomenal world is known as Prameya Chaitanya, or the Object Cognized.

That which knows is called *Pramâtâ* ; that which produces knowledge of an object is *Pramâna* ; and an object or thing knowable is called *Prameya*, In other words the qualified Âtmâ is the *knower* in one state, *knowledge* in the other, and a *thing known* in the third.

---

* Vide quotation No. 10.

According to Mimânsiks and Vedântists, there are six kinds of Pramânas (proofs or means of arriving at correct knowledge), *viz* :—

1. Pratyaksha Pramâna (प्रत्यक्ष प्रमाण) Perception ; what is cognizable by any of our senses.

2. Anumiti (अनुमितिः), Inference from given premises.

3. Shabda (शब्द) Right affirmation, or verbal authority.

4. Upmiti (उपमितिः), Comparison ; a knowledge of things derived from Analogy.

5. Arthâpatti (अर्थापत्ति) Presumption or supposition of a truth without positive proof. It is, in fact, the supposition of a thing although the thing itself is not perceived, but necessarily implied by another which is seen, heard, or proved ; it is an inference used to account for an apparent contradiction; for instance, when we say that one is fat but does not eat during the day, the apparent contradiction contained in this statement can only be accounted for by presuming that he 'eats' at night.

6. Anupalabdhi (अनुपलब्धिः) Non-realization of the fact; for instance, the knowledge of the absence of a pot is possible as the counter-fact does not exist with the negative state or Abhâva (अभाव).

The Sânkhya system recognizes only the first three kinds of proof, and the Nyâya system, the first four kinds only. The former thinks that the last three, and the latter thinks that the last two, are included in the first three or the first four respectively.

The knowledge acquired by the above Pramânas (proofs) is called Pramâ Jnâna or true knowledge, acquired by proper means. Knowledge acquired otherwise (for instance, imagination), is not Pramâ Jnâna, and is, therefore, not true knowledge.

Pratyaksha, which means express or direct, is of three kinds :—

1. Knowledge of self or self-consciousness,

2. Knowledge of ideas present in the mind, and

3. Knowledge of outward objects through the mind and senses.

In every cognition three things are always present, namely, the knower, the act of knowing, and the object known. The above might as well be expressed by saying that it denotes :--

1. Knower's knowledge of self existence ,

2. Knower's knowledge of the act of knowing ; and

3. Knower's knowledge of the object known.

We also find by experience (1) that the knower's knowledge of self existence is always persistent ; (2) that the kowner becomes conscious of his mental ideas directly, without any means or help; and (3) that the knower knows the outward objects through the instrumentality of the mind and the senses.

Avidyâ or ignorance.

The Avidyâ (Ne-Science or Ignorance) is the cause on account of which the subjective and objective phenomena appear to us in different forms. This Avidyâ is of two kinds ; one is called Mûlâ-Ajnâna, and the other Tûlâ-Ajnâna. The Mûlâ-Ajnâna envelopes the Âtmâ, and keeps it back from the knowledge of its own real self ; and the Tûlâ-Ajnâna is that which envelopes the Prameya-Chaitanya (knowable objects), and hides it from Pramâtâ-Chaitanya (the knower). The Pramâtâ-Chaitanya (knower) knows the different phenomena by removing the Tûlâ-Ajnâna of the different objects with the help of the different Pramânas (proofs): and by removing the Mûlâ-Ajnâna with the help of Shabda Pramâna (Right Affirmation) it comes to know its own self-existence.

How different objects are known.

Now we will first describe the way by which Tūlâ-Ajnâna is removed, and the Pramâtâ-Chaitanya becomes able to know the external objects. The mind within us is like the vast surface of an ocean. When the surface of an ocean is in motion, we call the phenomena thus produced, bubbles, ripples, waves, and so forth. Likewise, when a motion takes place in the surface of the mind, diffent ideas and thoughts arise, and we say we are thinking. As the bubbles, ripples, and waves are only a modification of the water, in the same way, the ideas and thoughts are only a modification of the mind.

It is the mind only, in its modified state, which passes through the five senses and perceives the outward objects. This modification of the mind is called in Sanskrit its Vritti. But it has already been stated that Âtmâ, the real entity, underlies all phenomena, both objective and subjective; and, therefore, whenever the mind and its modifications are spoken of, these terms always imply the existence of Âtmâ, or Real Entity, underlying the mind and its modifications. Now let us suppose there is a table before us: the earth being a dark planet sheds forth dark rays; and it is for this reason that everything on earth is enveloped in darkness. Now in order that I may be conscious of the existence of the table, it is required, in the first place, that the darkness enshrouding the table be removed with the help of light; be it of the sun, or moon, or electricity, or fire. In the next place, the eyes, which are the organs of visual perception, must be in a sound condition, then the mind which has the capacity of expansion, passes towards the object (in this instance the table) through the eyes and encircles it, and thus moulds itself into the shape of the table. As the light has the effect of removing the darkness, so the mind, in its modified state, called its Vrittis, has the effect of removing the ignorance (Tûlâ-Ajnâna) of the object, and its perception by Pramâtâ-Chaitanya is the consequence. But as already stated, we find by experience that the ideas of the mind, that is, its modifications, are known directly to Pramâtâ-Chaitanya; and, therefore, in the example just given, the mind moulded itself into the form of the table, and the Pramâtâ-Chaitanya, having the capacity of directly knowing the modifications of the mind, became conscious of the form of the table. This is how an outward object is cognized.

How self is known.

In the above process, which results in our becoming conscious of an outward object, two things are always present :—namely (1) that particular state of the object when it becomes knowable and (2) the modification of the mind that removes the veil of ignorance and makes the object known to Pramâtâ-Chaitanya (the knower). But in acquiring a knowledge of the mental ideas none of these are required as the ideas are directly known. We have seen that in the cognition of an outward object, the presence of Vritti is necessary, but to know a Vritti (an idea) itself, another Vritti (modification of mind) is not required, because here the Vritti itself is the object to be known, which is self-luminous, and is knowledge itself. We cannot, even for the sake of argument, suppose that one Vritti, is required to enable us to know another Vritti, as the supposition is impossible—because, the first Vritti disappears as soon as another Vritti takes its rise. The presence of two conflicting ideas at one and the same time is impossible. Therefore a Vritti, is not required to know another Vritti, just as a lighted candle is not required to see another lighted candle, which is self-luminous, and is necessary only to see an outward object. Thus the presence of a Vritti is required to know outward objects, but not to know another Vritti, which is itself knowledge, and knowable directly to Pramâtâ-Chaitanya. The Pramâtâ-Chaitanya is the real Power underlying the mind, and being the self of the mind, it is itself the witnesser of all phenomena, both objective and subjective.

When ideas arise, the Pramâtâ-Chaitanya appears as the knower, and when no ideas arise, the Pramâtâ-Chaitanya, although having the power of knowing, does not appear as such; for there is nothing present before it then which it may know.

In the same way to know one's own self, the presence of a Vritti is required. The Vritti acts to remove the Mûlâ-Ajnâna, which enveloped the Chaitanya, and kept it ignorant of its own self. As soon as the ignorance of self is removed, the knowledge of self takes its place. To repeat the same, as a lighted candle is not required to see another lighted candle, so no other Pramâtâ-Chaitanya is required to know a Pramâtâ-Chaitanya. The Pramâtâ-Chaitanya (knower), as we have already stated, is the witnesser and not a witnessed object, How can any one know the knower? When a Vritti arises in the mind, we find that an act of knowing takes place and a trinity is formed. There is a knower, there is a Vritti (idea) the object known, and there is the act of knowing. In the act of knowing the mental phenomena, the existence of the knower is signified by every modification of the mind, of which the knower becomes conscious; the knower's real existence which when not acting as knower is called in Sanskrit Âtmâ (the real self).

Having understood that there is only one Real Entity underlying all phenomena, one stands in need of a preceptor to know what that Entity is. The preceptor then initiates him into the mysterious science, by announcing the formula "That Reality, Thou art," and in consequence of this teaching, there arises a particular idea in the mind of the pupil, which he expresses by saying "I am that (Reality)." This idea removes the ignorance of the Pramâtâ-Chaitanya, which then realises itself as the "Reality," the self of all. In this act of knowing the Pramâtâ-Chaitanya recognizes itself as the knower and not as an object known; the object known being the idea that "I am that (Reality)."

Elucidation of the above truth by an illustration.

It would be better to elucidate here the above truth by an illustration of a mirror. According to Vedic Philosophy, the eye, on a small scale, is similar in its construction to the sun. So the functions of the former are similar on a microcosmic scale, to those of the latter. Such being the case, the Visual rays proceed from the eye as the rays of light proceed from the sun. The sun being the fountain-head of all light, the laws which govern its rays are exactly applicable to the rays of light of every description. In seeing an image in a mirror, the visual rays passing through the pupil fall on the surface of the mirror. These rays are reflected, making an angle of reflection equal to the angle of incidence. The transparency of the surface, and the back of the glass being silvered, cause the rays to revert and fall on the objects that go to form the angle of reflection. But, as already stated, it is the mind only that passes through the eye, and assumes the form of the object it comes into contact with; and it is this mental form of which the knower becomes conscious. Likewise, when we look at a mirror, the visual rays passing through the pupil fall on its surface, and, reverting, reflect on the face and other objects that form the angle of reflection, thus moulding themselves into the form of the face and other objects. But truly speaking, it is the mind that passes with the visual rays through the pupil, and of all the forms which it accepts and assumes the knower becomes conscious; in the case in point, for instance, it becomes conscious of the face and other objects that form the angle of reflection.

The theory of Science that by reflection of the rays of light a picture of outward objects is printed on the retina, and that the mind then in some mysterious manner becomes conscious of this, does not appear to be sound: because the retina on which the picture is supposed to be printed being itself so small an object, the picture must necessarily be but a miniature of the original, just as in the case of (portraits or views taken by the process of) photography. Scientific men are unable to explain how the mind becomes conscious by mere perception through so small an organ as the eye of the size of huge mountains and vast space, of which no real impression has actually been produced on the retina. The Vedic saying is, therefore, true, which informs us that the mind, passing with the visual rays, encompasses the objects with which it comes into contact, and causes the soul to become conscious of the form into which the mind moulds itself. This is amply proved in the example of the mirror, for we find that objects forming an angle of reflection are seen in their full size.

The eye, cannot see itself. To see itself it stands in need of a mirror ; the subject thus becoming the object of its own action. Similarly, to know itself, the Âtmâ requires a *Vritti* as the mirror is necessary for an eye to see itself.

Refutation of the objection of Messrs Mansel and Spencer regarding the knowledge of self.

The above explanation will clealy show that the objection raised by Mr. Mansel and adopted by Mr. Herbert Spencer (*vide* quotation No. 7) according to which the subject and the object are identified does not hold good, as the knower and the known do not become one; for here the knower knows itself as the knower of the idea present before it, and not as a known object. Thus, there is no annihilation of the knower and the known.

The difficulty under which Messrs. Mansel and Herbert Spencer appear to have laboured is, that they apparently tried to know '*Self*' like other objects. If '*Self*' be regarded like other objects, the objection of Mr. Herbert Spencer may hold good ; but if, as we hold, '*Self*' becomes conscious of itself, as the knower and not as the known, the objection falls to the ground. Thus, it will appear that there is a difference between the knowledge of 'Self' and of things that are not 'Self.' The Kena Upanishad of the Sâma Veda very clearly shows this distinction in the form of a dialogue between a disciple and a teacher, from which we give the following extract :—

KENA UPANISHAD, FIRST SECTION :—

1. " (The diciple asks) By whom willed and (by whom) appointed, does the mind speed (to its work) ? " By whom ordained does the first (Prâna) life breath proceed ? By whom willed is the speech pronounced ? Which God assigns their functions to the eye and ear ?"

2. " (The teacher answers) He who is the ear of the ear,

the mind of the mind, speech of the speech, is verily the life (breath) of the life (breath), the eye of the eye. The wise abandoning (the thought that the ear, the mind; the speech, the life breath and the eye have each an independent existence of their own) and, giving up the desires of this world, become immortal."

3. "Him (the Supreme Brahman) the eye does not approach, nor speech, nor mind. We do not recognize Him (as anything perceptible), therefore, we do not know how to teach his nature (to a disciple). It is even different from what is known (the Manifested Universe ; if you then say, it must be the Unmanifested Universe, no), it is also beyond what is not known (to the senses, it is beyond the Unmanifested Universe). Thus we heard from the teachers of old who explained this to us."

4. "Consider that which is not manifested by speech, but by which speech is manifested, to be the Brahman, and not what is worshipped as 'this' or 'that' (viz., any individual thing which is perceived) . . . .
. . . ."

Second Section.

1. "If thou thinkest*, I know (Brahma) well, (I say) what thou knowest of the nature of that Brahma, (with reference to the Adhyâtama or Individual Self) is, indeed, little : it is, indeed, little, what thou knowest of his nature with reference to the Adhidaiva or deities ; therefore, is Brahma to be further considered by thee."

* Dr. E, Röer, from whose translation I take the above extracts from Kena Upanishad (with certain modifications,) gives in the form of a foot-note the following remarks of S'ri S'ankarâchârya on this passage :—
"A pupil who has attentively followed the exposition which has been given on the nature of Brahma in the first section, is compelled to think that he knows Brahma perfectly. It is the well-defined meaning of all writings, on the Vedânta, that the Self or Soul of every one who knows, is Brahma. Further, the idea of Brehma is in this Upanishad introduced by the passage : "He who is the ear of the ear ;"—
"and firmly established by the passage : "That which is

2. " (The pupil says) I do not think I know Him ; by this I mean to say that I do not know Him well (as a perceptible object) ; and yet I do know Him (as taught by spiritual teachers by the tradition of the school). Whosoever amongst us understands my words :—"I do not know Him, yet I do know Him," knows Him (Brahma).

3. " By Him (the knower of Brahma), who thinks that Brahma is not comprehended (as an object of the sense or mind), Brahma is comprehended ; he, who (not knowing Brahma) thinks that Brahma is comprehended (as an object of the sense or mind), does not know Him. Brahma is unknown to those who (think they) know Him (as a perceptible object), and (is yet) known to those who do not (think they) know Him (as a perceptible object)."

4. " If He is known as the knower of every thought, He is comprehended (as the knower). Hence (from this knowledge) a person gains immortality. A person gains power by one's self, and by the knowledge of self, immortality." . . . .

Again, in Brihad Âranyaka Upanishad, we find that, in reply to a question from his wife Maitreyi, in reference to the knowledge of Âtmâ, the Rishi Yâjnavalkya said (Fourth Chapter, Fifth Brâhman, S'ruti 14):—" Behold, I verily do not create bewilderment ; behold this soul is indestructible ;

---

not manifested by speech, &c." Lastly the decision of the school of the Vedânta is given in the words :—" He is even different from what is known, &c." Notwithstanding these apparent reasons, the pupil is wrong in supposing that he has obtained a perfect (perceptible) knowledge of Brahma. Of everything which may become an object of knowledge, a perfect or definite (perceptible) knowledge is possible ; but not so of a thing which cannot become such an object. This is Brahma ; for he is the knower, and the knower may well know other things, but not make himself the object of his knowledge (or *if* we should render this in modern phraseology : The subject of knowledge, " I who know," can never become its object; for having become object, it ceases to have the nature of subject), in the same way as fire can burn other things but not itself. (What a contrast to the system of Fichte!) Nor can it be said, that Brahma may be made the object of the knowledge of another ; for beside him, none that knows exists."

its nature is without variance. For where there is, as it were, duality, there one sees another thing, smells another thing tastes another thing, speaks another thing, minds another thing, touches another thing, knows another thing ; but how does one, to whem all has become 'One' (Âtmâ), see any thing, how smell anything, how taste anything how hear any thing, how mind anything, how touch anything, how know anything? How should he know Him by whom he knows this all? This soul (Âtmâ) is not this, nor aught else; it is unseizable, for it cannot be seized; it is not scattered, for it cannot be scattered; it is without contact, for it comes not into contact; it is without colour ; it is not subject to pain or destruction. How should one know the knower? In this manner art thou instructed. So far, O beloved Maitreye, extends in truth immortality."

It was in this way that our Rishis of old realized the Âtmâ (self), and following in their footsteps, the we realize it even now.

The Absolute Nature of Âtmâ (self).

Mr. Herbert Spencer would here object and say that I am speaking of the Non-relative, Absolute Reality in relative terms, and an Absolute spoken of in relative terms is no Absolute at all. This objection would hold if we were to admit that the existence of the knower is destroyed with the absence of the objects known. In other words, this objection would amount to asserting that a tailor loses his existence when he is not working at his sewing machine. But this is not so. In the absence of an object the relation between the subject and the object is lost, but the existence of the subject is not destroyed. All thinkers would testify to the fact that there are moments when there is a cessation of all ideas. But apart from their evidence, it is in itself an apparent fact that the mind is blank when a change of ideas takes place, though this blank may be of very short duration, the conception of which is even difficult. I mean to say that when one thought subsides and another rises, then an absolute, though temporary blankness of mind must intervene. It is almost needless to say that there is no consciousness of any phenomena during sound sleep. When a cessation of ideas takes place, the Âtmà is not conscious, at the time, of anything; and there exists no relativity. Âtmâ (self) exists as Non-relative, and therefore Absolute. Will any one say that Âtmâ is annihilated at the time? If he does, it is not correct; for at the very next moment when fresh ideas arise it become conscious of them. The result is, that Âtmâ, really exists in its Absolute, Non-relative nature, even while there is a cessation of ideas. It appears to us in its Relative nature as the knower, when there exist objects to be known. This change of the aspect does not affect, in the least, the real nature of Âtmâ. The Upanishads allude to the Absolute, Non-relative Âtmâ in the following words:—

21. " This is his (true) nature (as found in sound sleep), which is free from desire, sin and fear. As in the embrace of a beloved wife one is unconscious of aught else, so, embraced by sound sleep, this Purusha is unconscious of all, without or within. This is his (true) nature, when all desires are satisfied, when the only desire is for self, where there is no desire, where there is no grief."

22. "Then, the father is no father, the mother is no mother, the worlds no worlds, the gods no gods, the Vedas no Vedas. Then the thief, is no thief, the murderer of a Brâhmana no murderer of a Brâhmana, the Chandâla no Chandâla, the Paulkasa no Paulkasa, the religious mendicant no religious mendicant, the ascetic no ascetic; he is unconnected with aught that is holy; he is unconnected with sin; for he is then beyond every grief of the heart.

23. "He sees not being thus (in profound sleep), (it is not (literally) true, for he does see), but while seeing, he sees not; for (actually) there is no loss of sight to the see-er since it has not been destroyed; but there is no second, no object separated from himself which he may see."

S'rutis 24 to 30 repeat the words of S'ruti 23 in regard to the act of smelling, tasting, speaking, hearing, minding, touching and knowing.

31. "Wherever some other thing (seemingly) appears to exist, there one may see another thing, smell another thing, taste another thing, speak (to or with) another thing, hear another thing, mind or touch something else, and know another thing."

32. "Like (pure) water, the one see-er exists, without duality. This (profound sleep) is the Brahma world, O King of Kings;" thus Yâjnavalkya instructed him. * "This is his highest aim, his highest wealth, his highest world, his highest bliss. Of this bliss all other beings enjoy only a part."

Brihad Âranyaka Upanishad, Chapter IV, Third Brâhmana.

SECTION XXIII.

"That which is Immensity is felicity, there is no felicity in Exiguity; Immensity alone is felicity; Immensity, therefore, is worthy of enquiry." "That Immensity, O Lord! (said Nârada to Sanat Kumâra), " is sought by me."

SECTION XXIV.

1. "Immensity is that of which none can see, of which none can hear, and of which none can know. Exiguity is that of which another can see, of which another can hear, and of which another can know. Verily, that which is Immensity is immortal and that which is Exiguity is mortal."

Chhandogya Upanishad, Chapter VII.

Benefit arising from the Knowledge of Self.

An agnostic might perhaps question at this stage the benefit likely to accrue from acquiring the knowledge of self; because he would say that the *real self*, whether one knows *It* or not, remains all along the same and unchanged, and that it would make no difference whether one knows *It* or remains ignorant of *It*, for, in both cases, Âtmâ is not in the least

* Janaka, the king of Videhas.

affected. This objection does not apyly to the case of a knower of self who having realized the Real Entity, finds himself immortal. While the case of an agnostic stands on a different footing. His standpoint is, that the Real Power is unknowable and thus, so far as the knowledge of self is concerned, an ignorant person and an agnostic, however learned, stand on the same footing. Both of them acknowledge without hesitation that they are unable to discern the Real Power underlying all the phenomena, as well as the phenomena, in their ultimate nature. I do not understand what satisfaction can one possibly obtain when he is ignorant of his own real self ; does not know what his end will be, and is not quite sure as to the ultimate nature of the relative realities.

It is altogeher otherwise in the case of a knower of Âtmâ (self). His Âtmâ certainly remains as it ever was, but his ignorance of self has been removed. It was only the ignorance of one's own real nature which caused him to believe that he was liable to pleasure and pain and life and death. But on acquiring the knowledge of Âtmâ (self) one comes to know that the Reality underlying all phenomena is his own *self* which is Indivisible, Finer than the Fine, Absolute, Infinite, Unchangeable, Self-conscious, and from which all the relative phenomenal world derives its existence. Is not, therefore, ignorance, the lot of an agnostic, a misery : and knowledge, the lot of a knower of self, a bliss ?

The knower of self is highly praised by the Upanishads. They, in fact, say. "that the knower of Brahma is Brahma Itself." I might give here several quatotions from the Upanishads bearing on the point, but I refrain from so doing as they will fill much space; and I would avoid, as far as possible, tiring the reader, who, however, if interested in the subject, will find little difficulty in referring to them in the original works, or to translations from which I have already made copious extracts.

Much praise is due to Swâmi Dayânanda Saraswati, whose teachings have, during the present age of Atheism and Materialism, roused once more the sleeping sons of Ârya-Varta to explore their Vedic mines of true knowledge. It was, indeed, the Grand Swâmi who stopped the torrent which was hurling down the youths of Modern India to Atheistic views or to religious Samajas which do not acknowledge the revelation of the holy Veda; and it is due to his efforts that those of our countrymen who are only conversant with languages other than Sanskrit and like manners foreign to us, have begun to look with reverence on the Vedas and Shâstras.

Swâmi Dayânanda Saraswati.

But with due deference to his scholarship and knowledge of the Vedas and Upanishads it may be said that he differed from the views of the Vedantins in believing in the Ultimate Absolute Existence of Matter (Prakriti), of Individual Soul (Jivâtmâ), and of God (I'shvara) separately instead of the existence of the one absolute Reality (Atman) and the former as Manifestations only. It is not understood how the Swâmi believed in the Omnipresence of God (I'shvara), when he at the same time believed in the Absolute and Independent Existence of each of the other two entities, *viz.*, Matter (Prakriti) and the Individual Soul (J'iva). How do the Ârya Samâjists meet the objection, that if Matter and Individual Souls, have separate respective independent existences of their own, how can their God remain omnipresent and all-pervading; they are bound to cripple Him logically and render Him a finite and conditioned I'shvara.

This objection does not apply to us who believe the Âtmâ to be the final and only cause of all the phenomena. Their (the Ârya Samâjist's) statement of the Omnipresence of Ether (Akâsha) in all the other elements, to prove the omnipresence of God, does not stand; because, the fact that it was from Ether that all the other elements evolved (as effects do from cause) is not denied by the Swâmi, and, therefore, as effects can never exist independently of their cause, the other elements exist in their cause, *viz.*, Ether, and hence the omnipresence of the latter in the former. But the Swami does not believe, in this sense, that the Matter and the Individual Souls are effects of I'shvara (God) (its cause). If he were to believe that God is the cause, and the Universe Its effects only, then his doctrine of the independent nature of Matter and Soul falls to the ground; because the cause in its own nature and as seen in its effects is really never changed. No difference takes place in the nature of gold if it is turned into ornaments, or if water is turned into ice, and so on. The Existence of the Trinity which the Swami preached is a relative and not an ultimate truth; and I would, therefore, exhort my brethren of Ârya-Samaj to try and find out the ultimate truth.

Madam Blavatsky and the Theosophical Society.

Great Praise is due to Madam H. P. Blavatsky, and Mrs. Anni Besant who, though of a foreign nation, did so much for the revival of Ancient Sanskrit Literature and Brahma-Vidyâ. Praise is also due to those members of the Theosophical Society, whose energies are inexhaustible in the search for the invaluable truths of the Ancient Âryan Literature, at present lying shadowed in darkness—lost however only to be regained, let us hope, by steadfastly continued research. A great impetus has been given by the Theosophical Society to the movement started by Swâmi Dayânanda Saraswati in the interests of the study of Ancient Sanskrit Literature.

My humble Advice to the Reader.

When so much has been done within the last twenty-five years by Swâmi Dayânanda Saraswati, Madam Blavatsky, Mrs. Anni Besant and the Theosophical Society, with the view of creating an interest in the study of Vedic Literature, I venture to advise my readers to try and fit themselves for the study of Brahma-Vidyâ. I trustfully venture to say that they will thus finally attain liberation from re-incarnation, by the realization of Self, which is the only Reality, the substratum of all appearances. I venture to express the hope that the reader will earnestly take the subject to heart, and studiously examine it for himself; and not lose the opportunity afforded him of removing the ignorance of Self, under which he is labouring. Thus too, says the Upanishad :—

KATHA UPANISHAD—SIXTH VALLI.

4. "If here (in this life) one is able to comprehend Him (Brahma) before the death of the body, he will be liberated from the bondage of the world; if one is not able to comprehend him he is destined to assume another body (in this world)."

KENA UPANISHAD—SECOND SECTION.

5. "If in the present incarnation a person knows the soul, then the true end (of all human aspiration) is gained, if a person in this present incarnation does not know the soul, there will befal him great calamity. The wise who discern in all beings oneness (the nature of Brahma), become immortal abandoning all desires of this world."

AUTHOR.

PART I.

PRELIMINARY ESSAYS.

ओम्

I.

THE EVOLUTION AND INVOLUTION OF THE WORLD.

आसीदिदं तमोभूतमप्रज्ञातमलक्षणम् ।
अप्रतर्क्यमविज्ञेयं प्रसुप्तमिव सर्वतः ॥

This (Universe) existed only (first in the Divine Idea, though yet unmanifested) in darkness, imperceptible, undefinable, incomprehensible and unknowable as if it were wholly enveloped in sleep. Manu Chapter I. śloka 5.

सूर्याचन्द्रमसौ धाता यथा पूर्वमकल्पयत ।
दिवं च पृथिवीं चान्तरिक्षमथो स्वः ॥

The Supreme Divinity formed the Sun, Moon, Lightning, Earth, Atmosphere &c., in the present just as He had formed them in the preceding cycle (Kalpa कल्प). Rig-Veda Mandala 10 Sukta 190 Mantra 3.

यदा स देवो जागर्ति तदेदं चेष्टते जगत् ।
यदा स्वपिति शान्तात्मा तदा सर्वं निमीलति ॥

When that Divinity awakes (for, though actual slumber as we use the word literally cannot be attributed to Brahman which is the root of all the roots and life and spirit of all the lives and spirits, yet it is figuratively used as a general property of life) then this Universe begins to manifest, but when He is wrapped up in deep slumber, then the whole system fades away. Manu Chapter I. śloka 52.

THE Earth we inhabit is a planet revolving round the Sun. The elements of which it is composed are classified by the Indian Philosophers under five main heads, *viz.*, solids, liquids, heat or luminous matter, gasses and ether named respectively in Sanskrit Prithvi (पृथ्वी) Apas (अपस्) Tejas तेजस्) Vâyu (वायु) and Akash (आकाश).

From our knowledge of the globe we inhabit and its environments we are in a position to infer that other heavenly bodies and planets are also composed of the said five elements. Though it is quite probable and even certain that the elements in the higher bodies might be of a finer nature than the elements of our globe, and also that in bodies like the Sun the element of lumnious matter (तेजस्) preponderates : but it may be observed that if any general principle be found applicable to the objects composed of the said five elements in this globe of ours, the same may well be considered to apply also to the rest of the universe, subject however, to modifications under different circumstances. These elements of which the material world is composed, when considered as a single whole are called in Sanskrit प्रकृति (Prakriti) or nature. This nature is known to us by its three qualities named Satwa, Rajas and Tamas. These words are differently translated into English and the best rendering appears to me to be Goodness or Lightness, Passion or Activity, and Darkness or Inertia respectively. Even the smallest conceivable particle of the material world, so often called an atom, manifests these three qualities. Thus it appears that every single atom has got within it the element of activity. It is for this reason that Science teaches us that the atoms of everything in the world whether living or apparently lifeless are in constant rapid motion.

We also find that the above named three qualities are never found in equal degree in any single object. There is always an increase or decrease in quantity of one quality over the other. We further find that all such objects have a capacity to produce certain effects, when the elements of which they are composed possess the said qualities or Gunas in certain proportionate degrees. We also know that this capacity gets exhausted after certain known effects have been produced and the same object becomes unable to produce any longer the same effects which it was once capable of producing and did actually produce under certain conditions. It therefore appears evident that either certain finer parts of the object have disappeared altogether from it, or that those parts have fallen out of order so as to render the object unfit for producing further effects such as those it had once produced. Then follows a period of rest, during which a reaction takes place and the dormant qualities each gradually and in proper time recover their former strength. Let us illustrate this by some examples. The cultivators of the soil inform us that culturable wastes, when broken up, yield luxuriant crops as compared with lands already cultivated : but if we continue to sow the same land at every harvest, its productive powers gradually decrease till at last it fails to produce altogether. This shows that either some of its finer parts have disappeared altogether or become so weak and deranged that the soil is rendered perfectly unfit for further production. In order that the same soil may again be able to produce the crops it once did, it requires in the ordinary course of nature a rest from further cultivation. To manure the land is an artificial method of helping the soil to recoup its strength in a comparatively shorter time than it would otherwise have done. Now let us leave alone for a moment the question of artificial help. Wise cultivators grow different crops by turns, and always leave the land uncultivated either for a single harvest or more, according to the strength of the soil. Experience also tells us that the productive powers of lands which have been under cultivation for a long period fail to produce a sufficiency of crops and it is for this reason that old villages have often been deserted altogether and new ones sprung up in places where the people have been able to find culturable lands to break up. It, therefore, clearly follows that by taking a crop out of a plot of land the latter loses a part of its strength either by the disappearance of its finer parts or by their derangement or by both. The only way to restore its strength is to give it rest for a while, that is to say not to grow crops upon it for a certain period of time so as to enable a reaction to take place. The same power of producing and non-producing is seen in fruit trees which bear abundant fruits at one season and produce less during the succeeding season and so on, till the power of production is entirely exhausted. The same process of action and reaction also takes place in the animal kingdom. We find that bodily labor exhausts bodily strength and mental labor exhausts mental capacity for work. Physical rest recoups physical strength and mental rest restores the mental faculties, this is observable in daily life ; a man is engaged to dig a ditch, he gets tired and is unable to raise the hoe for further work but when he takes a little rest he is again fit for work. Likewise when a man feels himself tired of study or contemplation he goes to sleep for a while or otherwise takes rest for a time and soon afterwards finds himself refreshed and ready to begin his work with renewed zeal and vigour of mind. The incapacity for further work is a proof of the soil and man having lost some fine parts as well as that these have become so deranged as to make them unfit for further work. Rest alone or artificial help either in the shape of manure, medicine, food or diet, given for the purpose of supplying the lost strength restores the power which they formerly possessed ; and this process of action and reaction, of arrangement or capacity to perform a thing and derangement or incapacity to perform it, and consequent rearrangement will be found going on without interruption in the matter composing the material world. It is true that in producing an effect, as well as in regaining the lost strength so as to be again able to produce an effect, there is motion all along existing ; but I take the liberty of using the word motion here only in its limited sense confining its meaning to the state of a thing when it is actually exercising its capacity to produce an effect, whereas I will call it a cessation of motion when there is a want of power to produce an effect, and when the process of recouping is going on. Taking the words *motion* and *cessation of motion* in the sense above indicated, I am entitled to say that the things of the universe appear to us in two aspects *viz.*, motion and cessation of motion. These two conditions apply only to the different and multifarious objects of which this universe is composed, but these cannot be said to apply in the same sense to the universe itself as a whole in its present state : because, the universe at present in the onward course of its cyclic evolution is bringing forth into manifestation all its powers and strength of production. The universe as a whole in its present state may therefore be said to be in motion in the sense defined above. But we have seen that the matter of which the universe is composed, shows two conditions, namely motion and cessation of motion, or in other words, manifestation of certain effects as well as their eventual disappearance. We always judge the whole from the parts or parts from the whole. Therefore the general principles that apply to the whole will also apply to the parts, and those that are found to apply to the parts will also surely apply to the whole. If the universe considered as a whole displays only the aspect of motion, as it surely does, it necessarily follows that there must come a time when the capacity to manifest the different effects it now holds, will be exhausted, and the universe as a whole will require rest to regain its lost strength in order to enable itself to appear again in freshness and full vigour, to manifest the different effects as it now does.

There is also another strong reason, based on our daily experience, proving the dissolution of the world. To find whether the world is liable to dissolution or not, we must know the component parts of which the world is made up. Leaving aside the discussions of the philosophers as to the matter of which the world is composed, we find that every material thing can be separated into pieces as small as atoms. These atoms, when combined, form the thing, and their separation from one another means disintegration and dissolution of the thing. There is no reason therefore to entertain doubt as to the formation of the world by the combination of small particles or atoms. But if we find a thing made up of several parts, we naturally conclude that the component parts must at sometime have been in a separate state, and that they have subsequently combined under certain influences and formed themselves into a body. No man would consider on seeing a house made up of bricks, mortar, wood and iron that it had existed in that state from eternity. If we know that bricks or stones are a separate thing, mortar a separate thing, wood a separate thing and iron a separate thing we are naturally in a position to say that there must have been a time when these things had separately existed before the formation of the building. In the same way when we find that the universe is composed of separate parts and each part is formed of different elements and that each element is composed of the smallest particles or atoms we come to the conclusion that there must have been a time when these atoms existed separately. But the structure of the universe bears evidence at the same time, that each of its parts is undergoing a dissolution and a reformation. The world we have seen is composed of the so called atoms, which existed separately before the present manifestation came into existence and we must assuredly understand that these will again be separated and that consequently the world will fall into dissolution. The very combination of the component parts is a proof of the world's previous and future dissolution The time during which the universe manifests itself in various ways is called in Sanskrit Utpatti (उत्पत्ति) or development and the time when there is a cessation of motion and the universe undergoes a dissolution is called Pralaya (प्रलय) or final dissolution. The cycle or period during which the universe continues to exist in a manifested state is called Kalpa (कल्प) which consists of 4320 millions of years ; at the end of this period universal dissolution takes place and everything then remains in a state of chaos or unmanifested state for an equal period of time. During this period the universe recoups its capacity, and at the end of the said period again an evolution takes place and the formation of the world in its manifested state comes into existence. This process of evolution and involution goes on ad-infinitum in the universe as a whole. The following extract* from the Institutes of Manu, Chapter I, shows the different measures of time.

61. 'From this Manu named Swayambhuva (or sprung from the self existing), came six descendents, other Manus, (or perfectly understanding the scripture), each giving birth to a race of his own all exalted in dignity eminent in power ;

62. 'Swárochísha, Auttami, Támasa, Raivata, likewise Chacshusha, beaming with glory, and Vaivaswata, child of the sun.

63. 'The seven Manus (or those first created, who are to be followed by seven more) of whom Swayambhuva is the chief, have produced and supported this world of moving and stationary beings, each in his own Antara, or the period of his reign.

64. 'Eighteen 'nimeshas'; (or twinklings of an eye) are one 'Kásthá' ; thirty Káshthás, one 'Kalá' ; thirty Kalás, one 'muhurta' ; and just so many muhurtas, let mankind consider as the duration of their day and night.

65. 'The Sun causes the distribution of day and night both divine and human ; night being (intended) for the repose of (various) beings and day for their exertion.

66. 'A month (of mortals) is day and night of the "Pitris" (or patriarchs inhabiting the moon) ; and the division (of a month) being into equal halves, the half beginning from the full moon is their day for action ; and that beginning from the new moon is their night for slumber.

---

*The translation of Manu's S'lokas given in this treatise is taken from The Popular Edition of Manu's Institutes of Hindu Law translated by Sir William Jones, Judge of Her Majesty's Supreme Court, Bengal.

67. 'A year (of mortals) is a day and a night of the Gods, (or regents of the universe seated round the north pole) ; and again their division is this : their day is the northern, and their night the southern course of the Sun.

68. 'Learn now the duration of a day and a night of Brahmá and of the several ages, which shall be mentioned in order succinctly.

69. 'Sages have given the name of 'Crita' to an age containing four thousand years of the gods ; the twilight preceding it consists of as many hundreds and the twilight following it, of the same number :

70. 'In the other three ages ; with their twilight preceding and following, are thousands and hundreds diminished by one.

71. 'The divine years, in the four (human) ages just enumerated, being added together, their sum, (or) twelve thousand, is called the age of the Gods ;

72. 'And by reckoning a thousand such divine ages, a day of Brahmá may be known : his night also has an equal duration :

73. 'Those persons best know the divisions of days and nights, who understand, that the day of Brahmá, which endures to the end of a thousand such ages, gives rise to virtuous exertion ; and that his night endures as long as his day.

74. 'At the close of his night, having long reposed, he awakes, and, awaking, exerts intellect, or (reproduces the great principle of animation), whose property it is to exist unperceived by sense :

75. 'Intellect called into action by his will to create worlds, performs (again) the work of creation, and thence (first) emerges the subtile ether, to which philosophers ascribe the quality of conveying) sound ;

76. 'From ether, effecting a transmutation in form, springs the pure and potent air, a vehicle of all scents ; and air is held endued with the quality of touch.

77. 'Then from air, operating a change, rises light or fire; making objects visible, dispelling gloom, spreading bright rays and it is declared to have the quality of form.

78. 'But from light, a change being effected, comes water with the quality of taste ; and from water in the same way comes earth with the quality of smell ; such were they created in the beginning.

79. 'The before mentioned age of the Gods, or twelve thousand (of their) years, being multiplied by seventy-one, (constitutes what) is here named a Manavantra, (or the reign of a Manu.)

80. 'There are numberless Manavantras ; also creations and destructions of worlds, (innumberable) : the Being supremely exalted performs all this, (with as much ease as if in sport) again and again (for the sake of conferring happiness).'—

Division of Time.

18	Nimeshas	=	1 Kâshthâ. ($1\frac{3}{5}$ seconds).
30	Kâshthâs	=	1 Kalâ. (48 seconds).
30	Kalâs	=	1 Muhurta. (24 minutes).
60	Muhurtas	=	1 Day and night.
30	Days and nights	=	1 Month.
12	Months	=	1 Year (Human).
1	Year (Human)	=	1 Day and night of the Gods.
360 360	Human years or Divine days & nights	=	1 year of the Gods.

4000	Years of the Gods	or 14,40,000	human years	=	1 Krita yuga.
3000	Do.	or 10,80,000	Do.	=	1 Treta "
2000	Do.	or 7,20,000	Do.	=	1 Dwâpara "
1000	Do.	or 3,60,000	Do.	=	1 Kali "
2000	Do.	or 7,20,000	Do.	=	Sandhis or intervals of Junction.

Total 12,000 years of the Gods } = Four human Chatur yugas or an age of the Gods.

4320 Millions of Human years or 1000 Divine ages	=	One Kalpa or Day of Brahmâ. The night of Brahmâ has also an equal duration.
1 Age of the Gods multiplied by 71	=	1 Manavantra.

14 Manavantras = 1 Maha Manavantra or Kalpa. In each Manavantra there are 71 Chatar Yugas. This Kali Yuga is the 28th Yuga under the reign of Vyvaswata the seventh Manu who reigns over this Manavantra. At the end of a Manavantra a deluge takes place and the Manu who rescues different species in an ark becomes the ruler of the next Manavantra.

II.

RE-INCARNATION OF THE CONSCIOUS SOUL (JÎVÂTMÂ).

शुभाशुभफलं कर्म मनोवाग्देहसंभवम् ।
कर्मजा गतयो नृणामुत्तमाधममध्यमाः ॥ ३ ॥

Action either mental, verbal, or physical bears good or evil fruit, (according as it is good or evil), and from the actions of men proceed their various states of re-incarnation, the highest, the medium, and the lowest. Manu, Chapter XII S'loka 3.

THE theory inculcated in the above s'loka forms the basis of the doctrine of re-incarnation of souls, upon which are founded the systems of different religions and philosophies of the ancient Aryans of India. Although in the present age, India has well nigh forgotten the philosophic and Vedic truths once so familiar to her sons before the barbarous horde had devastated the sacred soil and destroyed her invaluable treasure, still all classes of persons either professing the vedic religion, or following any of the systems of Aryan Philosophy, firmly believe that in their present incarnation, they are constrained to enjoy the fruits of actions performed by them in their previous lives, and that all the occurrences, so often called accidents by ignorance, are but the results of their previous actions started by them by and through their body, speech and mind. To the Indian Philosophers who believe in Karma theory the difference of positions in life and experience of pleasure and pain are not the decrees of an autocratic, unjust and personal God, ho in order to please himself causes one to be born blind, another a leper and a third the son of a street beggar, while the same God allows others to be born in sound health and in high stations of life.

Let us see how far the principle so clearly demonstrated by Manu and believed by Vedic followers stands the test of reason

It is an undisputed theory of Science that motion once started never ceases, but, if unobstructed, continues to eternity. When any thing in motion ceases to move, it simply means that it transmits its motion to something else with which it comes into contact, while the latter receives the motion thus imparted and begins to move on : if it does not take into itself the whole of the motion thus communicated, the object originally in motion retracts.

From our own experience of action we know that motion implies volition, that is to say, where there is motion, there must be at its root a thought, then a desire, next a power of will, and lastly a Volition : and where there is thought there must necessarily follow motion : thus the motion immediately preceded by volition means the performance of an act.

We are now to see how far the above principles apply to us in our daily life—we find that we have got a physical body formed of what are commonly known as elements and consisting of different organs.

It appears that the external organs of this physical body work and act more or less according to the direction, and under the control of some inner principle more subtile and finer in nature than the organs themselves. This is known by the name of the inner organ or the mental Power or Powers. But though the motion of the physical body is thus dependent on the mental powers, we find that the physical motion has also a wonderful effect on the functions of the human mind (mental powers), as will be seen hereafter.

The next thing to be known is whether the functions of the mind are themselves independent in their own action. We, however, find that when we want to concentrate our whole attention on one subject, for instance reading, hearing, or seeing &c., the mind begins, in spite of itself, to think of something different as if compelled to do so by a superior influence acting from within.

Thus it appears that there is a third Inner Force more subtile than the human mind, and this is called the Conscious Soul (Jîvátmá). But it may be observed that although the mind appears to be under the control and supremacy of the Inner Self or the Conscious Soul, we find (as it will be shown hereafter) that the actions of the mind itself have also a wonderful effect on the Conscious Soul. We will illustrate the above theory by three circles—each circle being linked with the other, and where the first circle ends, the second begins and where the second ends the third begins. The physical body in this illustration is denoted by circle A, the mind or the mental powers by circle B, and lastly the Conscious Soul by circle C. The first two circles are made up of parts. The third circle is a compact mass where the motions transferred remain in an obscure (unmanifested) state.

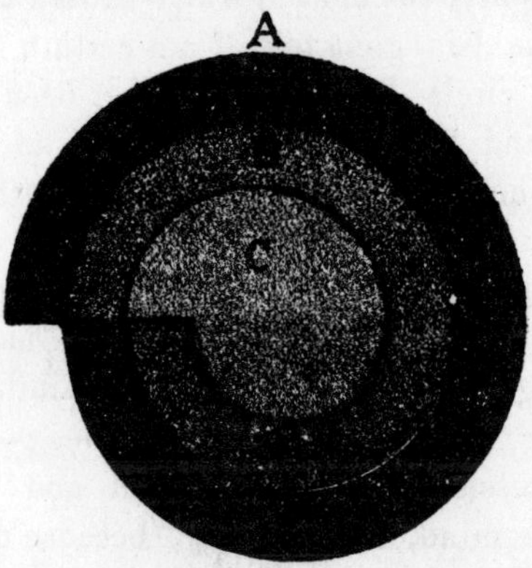

A careful analysis of our daily acts in life explains very clearly the theory of the above illustration. For instance, I find Devadatta who has fallen from his horse senseless on the ground. I at once run to his help, lift him up, remove the dust off his body and perform all acts necessary to

N.B.—If a rapid circular, twisting motion be given to this page, for about a minute to the right, the quasi circles on the said page will revolve, and the motion of the outer circles will appear to enter the inner ones in their respective order, and if similarly, motion be given to the left, the motion of the inner circles will be seen passing to the outer ones respectively.

cause Devadatta recover his strength. Leaving aside the result which my acts both mental and physical have on Devadatta, I find that they also cause a change of effect to take place in my mind. When the motion caused in the physical circle by lifting and giving other necessary help to Devadatta ceases, I feel a soothing and gratifying impression in my mind which in our illustration means that when the vibrations of the physical circle A, appear to come to a standstill, the vibrations of the mental circle B (which is in contact with the outer circle A) commence. But I find that for sometime all the ideas remain vivid in my mind, and after a while they disappear. Now the question is :—Where the motion which caused the vibrations in the mental circle has gone to? I am certain that it has not stopped in the circle B, because had it been so, the impressions on the mind would have continued to remain as vivid as they were when the action was first performed or when the occurrence is remembered. Nor can it be said that these impressions, by which I mean the motion transferred from the physical to the mental circle, have ceased altogether and gone to destruction or annihilation, as this is quite impossible for the following reasons :—First, because the same impressions are remembered and once more appear vivid in the mind, and secondly, because nothing goes to destruction. The principle enunciated at the outset was, that motion once produced never ceases and the object put in motion will move on for ever until its motion is transferred to another object, which in its turn begins to move on; or if the object in motion comes in contact with a thing which does not take into itself the whole of the motion, then it simply reverts; as a ball thrown on the ground rises up again. In our body we find that the mind when attentive to the motions of the physical body has the quality of transferring to itself the vibrations of the latter; but when otherwise occupied *i. e.* not attentive to the motions of the physical body it causes them to revert. In case of reversion we do not find a reaction of the mental vibrations on the physical plane nor do we find that they act on the mental plane; thus the effect which would have been produced is not produced and the sensitiveness of the circles A and B is not affected, or rather remains inoperative. But in the example of Devadatta we have shown that the motion of the physical plane has been transferred to the mental plane and that after a while it disappears from the latter plane without reverting to the physical plane, it therefore follows that the mental circle has in its turn transferred the motion to that of the Conscious Soul. As the vibrations of this circle are unknown to the mind, the impressions that go to this circle from the circle of the mind are said to go to forgetfulness.

There now arise two questions in the mind of the Inquirer. (1) Is the circle of the Conscious Soul the final circle and are there no further inner circles? and (2) If this be the final circle, do the impressions on this circle adhere to it for ever? The answer to the first question I would give in the affirmative and to the second in the negative. Persons who are or have been students, thinkers or Yogins (those who concentrate their mind in meditation) perfectly know what a great struggle is always going on in their minds. The student, the thinker, and the maditator at times find it next to impossible to check and control the different thoughts which arise within their mind in spite of themselves. We sit with a firm resolution to study a book or meditate on an object and we find of a sudden that we remember a thing which occurred some years ago. The mind is compelled to leave alone the object of its thought or meditation and to accept in its place the vivid impression which now stands before it unmoved. The question is, Whence does this impression come? It is not a new one nor a compound, but only the simple remembrance of a thing which occurred some years ago. When the thing occurred it made a vivid impression on the mind and was subsequently effaced therefrom and forgotten. After some years without any wish or attempt to recall to memory or without any association of ideas, the same occurrence recurs to the mind. This shows that the impressions which passed to the third circle revert to the second and that the third circle is the final circle. Had this circle been infinite there would have been no recurrence of thought as shown above. But as our mind and senses do not reach the third circle, we are not in a position to say that there are any sub-circles in it. We have observed old occurrences recurring; therefore we say that the impressions in the third circle do not adhere to it for ever. The third circle of the Conscious Soul is called in Sanskrit Jivátmá as well as Vija or seed. The reason why it is called seed is, that it becomes the cause of the motion in the mind and the motion in the mind if not reverted to the circle of the Conscious Soul, becomes in its turn the cause of the motion of the grosser circle, or rather of the performance of a physical act.

From the above it follows, that physical acts produce certain impressions on the mind and mental acts on the higher plane of the Conscious Soul. There being no further inner plane than that of the Conscious Soul, reversion of motion takes place and the result follows that the impressions which had been transferred to the third circle reflect on the mind, and the mind reacts on the body and the body moves to perform physical acts; thus there is a circulation of motion in the three circles. The middle circle sometimes reverts the motion to the circle from which it received it ; for instance, it reverts the impressions received through the senses, when it is otherwise occupied; as well as when Vijnána (the deciding faculty, which occupies a plane immediately higher in the mental powers next to the circle of the Conscious Soul) refuses to admit and transfer to the mental and physical circle, the impressions which it received from the third circle, (Conscious Soul). When this takes place then there is a communication of motion only between the first two or the last two of the circles. But when the motion of the first circle reaches the third or that of the third reaches the first, then a circulation of motion takes place; thus one act becoming the seed or the cause of another act of the same nature. It may also be mentioned that the impressions which reach the third circle arrange themselves in the form of a separate compound seed, that is to say, that each impression on the Conscious Soul has the effect of giving a new shape to the pre-existing compound, as the addition of a single medicine to a compound one changes its whole character and forms a new compound.

Having seen the circulation of motion in each of the three circles and its continuation, how foolish it would seem to say that there would be no recurrence of the impressions transferred to the Conscious Soul or, in other words, no reaping of the fruits of our actions. And we find that a seed when sown grows into a tree and the tree when full grown produces fruits which have seeds in them. These in their turn become the cause of new trees which again produce new fruits bearing seeds. A seed, is sure, under certain conditions, to spring up to a tree. What we call death, in our experience of this world, is the dissolution of the physical body. We are now to see whether with the dissolution of the grosser body the subtler one also dissolves. The answer is in the negative. Our reason for this answer is, that in a dream the mind acts perfectly independent of the physical body and in sound sleep the Conscious Soul exists independent of the mind and body, but the body never works independently of the mind and the Conscious Soul. By this, we mean to say that the grosser body is dependent for its existence on the mental body and the mental body is dependent for its existence on the Conscious Soul. If, therefore, the outer circle is dissolved, it does in no way affect the inner circles, which are in fact the soul of the outer circle. It is for this reason, that with the departure of the inner subtile bodies, the outer one or the grosser cover dies away. This theory is most elaborately explained in detail in Taittareya Upanishad; where it is stated, that there are five covers or sheaths by which the Higher Self is enshrouded. The first cover is a body of grosser element called Annamaya Kosha (अन्नमयकोश). This body depends for its existence on the Vital air called Mâtrishvâ, the action of which constitutes breathing and the other motions in the body

Mâtrishvâ is the Vital portion of our physical body. So long as this Vitality exists and holds together the different molecules of the grosser body, we are said to be living but when Vitality deserts the grosser body, the latter becomes a dead mass. This Mâtrishvâ is a refined prototype of the grosser body, a model, on which the latter depends for its existence. This second sheath of the Vital air is called Prânamaya Kosha (प्राणमयकोश).

We know further that there is a more subtle form of matter within this sheath of Prânamaya Kosha which is called Manomaya Kosha (मनोमयकोश) or the mental sheath: this is more subtle and refined than the second sheath, in as much as the property of the air is motion, and in the first sheath, the motion is physical, in the second it is physiological, and in the third it is perceived in the form of ideas, which consequently is more subtle than the first two.

The actions of the mind depend in their turn on the faculty which decides between good and bad and is a director over the mental powers. When this faculty is absent the mental powers disperse as an army disperses without a commander. This faculty is still finer and subtler; it is the essence of the third cover. The third cover is dependent on this directing faculty which is the fourth cover called Vijnânamaya-Kosha.

The fourth cover itself is dependent for its existence on the fifth which is of Bliss, called Ânandamaya Kosha. This fifth cover is that of the Conscious Soul or the Jivâtmâ. Each of the inner circles forms the essence of the outer or compartively grosser circle. It is the grosser that depends for its existence on the finer and inner circle and not the latter on the former, though the inner is dependent for its manifestation on the grosser and the outer circle.

What is stated above can be realized by making an experiment on all material objects. Everything has a grosser body which depends for its existence on the finer and inner body, which exists separately from the grosser body, though to a common observer there is no distinction between the two. But the studious observer knows better; as the chemist for example understands how to extract the essence from the grosser body with which he has to deal; and when the essence has been extracted the grosser body becomes worthless and is thrown away as rubbish. Likewise, the four inner circles exist separately of the physical body as does the essence of medicine or the oil of seeds exist separately from the object or seed itself. The chemist knows that the essence and the oil are separate from the grosser body which contains it. Likewise the philosopher knows that the inner subtle bodies exist independently of the grosser body, and that it is the grosser body that decays and is treated as useless when the inner ones are separated from it and which do not go to destruction. Hence we say that the dissolution of the grosser body only takes place at death, and the Ego (Conscious Soul) enveloped in mental powers continues to exist in the shape to which it has been moulded with the last impression it received during the continuance of the body. As is the seed so becomes the tree. Whatever impressions the Ego had received from the formations and re-formations of its past Karma (actions), it will surely manifest the same when it springs forth again. It is impossible for a seed to be buried under ground and not to germinate unless there are counteracting causes at work under certain conditions. Likewise, the Ego enveloped in ignorance and buried in the cover of the mental circle, must develop into a body of a superior or inferior nature as a seed does into a tree. The grosser body will be moulded according to the kind and nature of the seed from which it springs. This explains the theory of the Re-incarnation of the Ego. The rules according to which the Conscious Soul undergoes different births are very clearly given in Manu's Institutes, Chapter XII, from which I give the following extracts :—

3. 'Action, either mental, verbal, or corporeal, bears good or evil fruit, (as it is good or evil) ; and from the actions of men proceed their various transmigrations in the highest, the middle, and the lowest degree :—

4. 'Of that threefold action, connected with bodily functions, disposed in three classes, and consisting of ten orders, be it known in this world, that the mind is the instigator.

5. 'Devising means to appropriate the wealth of other men, resolving on any forbidden deed, and conceiving notions of atheism or materialism, are the three bad acts of the mind :

6. 'Scurrilous language, falsehood, indiscriminate backbiting and useless tattle, are the four bad acts of the tongue.

7. 'Taking effects not given, hurting sentient creatures without the sanction of law, and criminal intercourse with the wife of another, are the three bad acts of the body ; (and all the ten have their opposites, which are good in an equal degree).

8. ' A rational creature has a reward or a punishment for mental acts, in his mind; for verbal acts, in his organs of speech; for corporeal acts, in his bodily frame.

9. 'For sinful acts mostly corporeal, a man shall assume (after death) a vegetable or mineral form ; for such acts mostly verbal, the form of a bird or a beast; for acts mostly mental, the lowest of human conditions:

10. 'He, whose firm understanding obtains a command over his words, a command over his thoughts, and a command over his whole body, may justly be called a 'Tridandi', (or triple Commander, not a mere anchoret, who bears three visible staves).

11. 'The man, who exerts this triple self-command with respect to all animated creatures, wholly subduing both lust and wrath, shall by those means attain beatitude.

12. 'That substance, which gives a power of motion to the body, the wise call (cshetrajna, or Jivâtman) the vital spirit; and the body, which thence derives active functions, they name Bhûtâtman, or composed of elements :—

13. 'Another internal spirit, called (mahat) or the great soul, attends the birth of all creatures embodied, and thence in all mortal forms is conveyed a perception either pleasing or painful.

14. 'Those two, the vital spirit and rational soul, are closely united with five elements, but connected with Supreme Spirit, or divine essence, which pervades all beings high and low.

15. 'From the Substance of that supreme are diffused, (like sparks from fire), innumerable vital spirits, which perpetually give motion to creatures exalted and base.

16. 'By the vital souls of those men, who have committed sins, (in the body reduced to ashes), another body, composed of (nerves with) five senses, in order to be susceptible of torment, shall certainly be assumed after death;

17 'And being intimately united with those minute nervous particles, according to their distribution, they shall feel in that new body, the pangs inflicted in each case by the sentence of Yama.

18. 'When the vital soul has gathered the fruit of sins which arise from a love of sensual pleasure, but must produce misery, and, when its taint has thus been removed, it approaches again those two most effulgent essences (the intellectual soul and the divine spirit):

19. 'They two, closely conjoined examine without remission the virtues and vices of that sensitive soul, according to its union with which it acquires pleasure or pain in the present and future worlds.

20. 'If the vital spirit had practised virtue for the most part and vice in a small degree, it enjoys delight in celestial abodes, clothed with a body formed of pure elementary particles;

21. 'But, if it had generally been addicted to vice, and seldom attended to virtue, then shall it be deserted by those pure elements, and, (having a coarser body of sensible nerves), it feels the pains to which Yama shall doom it:

22. 'Having endured those torments according to the sentence of Yama, and its taint being almost removed, it again reaches those five pure elements in the order of their natural distribution.

23. 'Let each man, considering with his intellectual powers these migrations of the soul according to its virtue or vice, (into a region of bliss or pain), continually fix his heart on virtue.

24. 'Be it known, that the three qualities of the rational soul are a tendency to goodness, to passion, and to darkness; and endued with one or more of them, it remains incessantly attached to all these created substances:

25. 'When any one of the three qualities predominates in a mortal frame, it renders the embodied spirits, eminently distinguished for that quality.

26. 'Goodness is declared to be true knowledge; darkness, gross ignorance; passion, an emotion of desire or aversion; such is the compendious description of those qualities, which attend all souls.

27. 'When a man perceives in the rational soul a disposition tending to virtuous love, unclouded with any malignant passion, clear as the purest light, let him recognise it as the quality of goodness.

28. 'A temper of mind, which gives uneasiness and produces disaffection, let him consider as the adverse quality of passion, ever agitating embodied spirits:

29. 'That indistinct, inconceivable, unaccountable disposition of mind naturally sensual, and clouded with infatuation, let him know to be the quality of darkness.

30. 'Now will I declare at large the various acts, in the highest, middle, and lowest degrees, which proceed from those three dispositions of mind.

31. 'Study of scripture, austere devotion, sacred knowledge, corporeal purity, command over. the organs, performance of duties, and meditation on the divine spirit, accompany the good quality of the soul:

32. Interested motives for acts, (of religion or morality), perturbation of mind on slight occasions, commission of acts forbidden by law, and habitual indulgence in selfish-gratifications, are attendant on the quality of passion:

33. 'Covetousness, indolence, avarice, detraction, atheism, omission of prescribed acts, a habit of soliciting favours, and inattention to necessary business, belong to the dark quality.

34. 'Of those three qualities, as they appear in the three times, (past, present, and future), the following in order from the lowest may be considered as a short but certain criterion.

35. 'Let the wise consider, as belonging to the quality of darkness, every act, which a man is ashamed of having done, of doing or of going to do:

36. 'Let them consider, as proceeding from the quality of passion, every act, by which a man seeks exaltation and celebrity in this world, though he may not be much afflicted, if he fails in attaining his object:

37. 'To the quality of goodness belongs every act, by which he hopes to acquire divine knowledge, which he is never ashamed of doing and which brings placid joy to his conscience.

38. 'Of the dark quality, as described, the principal object is pleasure; of the passionate, wordly prosperity; but of the good quality, the chief object is virtue; the last mentioned objects, are superior in dignity.

39. 'Such transmigrations, as the soul procures in this universe by each of those qualities I will now declare in order succinctly.

40. 'Souls, endued with goodness, attain always the state of deities; those filled with ambitious passions, the condition

of men; and those immersed in darkness, the nature of beasts: this is the triple order of transmigration.

41. 'Each of those three transmigrations caused by the several qualities, must also be considered as three-fold, the lowest, the middle and the highest, according to as many distinctions of acts and of knowledge.

42. 'Vegetable and mineral substances, worms, insects, and reptiles, some very minute, some rather large, fish, snakes, tortoises, cattle, shackal, are the lowest forms, to which the dark quality leads:

43. 'Elephants, horses, men of the servile class, and contemptible Mlechhas, or barbarians, lions, tigers, and boars, are the middle states procured by the quality of darkness:

44. 'Dancers and singers, birds, and deceitful men, giants and blood thirsty savages, are the highest conditions, to which the dark quality can ascend.

45. 'Phallas, or cudgel players, Mallas, or boxers and wrestlers, Natas, or actors, those who teach the use of weapons, and those who are addicted to gaming or drinking, are the lowest forms occasioned by the passionate quality:

46. 'Kings, men of the fighting class, domestic priests of kings, and men skilled in the war of controversy, are the middle states caused by the quality of passion:

47. 'Gandharvas, or aerial musicians, Ruhyacas and Yacshas or servants and companions of Cuvera, genii attending superior Gods, as the Vidyâdharas and others, together with various companies of Apasarâs or nymphs, are the highest of those forms, which the quality of passion attains.

48. 'Hermits, religious mendicants, other Brahmins, such orders of demigods as are wafted in airy cars, genii of the signs and lunar mansions, and Daityas, or the offspring of Diti, are the lowest of states procured by the quality of goodness:

49. 'Sacrificers, holy sages, deities of the lower heaven, genii of the Vedas, regents of stars (not in the paths of the sun and moon), divinities of years, Pitris or progenitors of mankind, and the demigods named Sunhyas are the middle forms, to which the good quality conveys all spirits moderately endued with it:

50. 'Brahmâ with four faces, creators of worlds (under him, as Marichi and others), the genius of virtue, the divinities presiding over (two principles of nature in the philosophy of Capila) Mahat, or the mighty, and 'Avyacta,' or unmanifested, are the highest conditions, to which, by the good quality, souls are exalted.

51. 'This triple system of transmigrations, in which each class has three orders, according to actions of three kinds, and which comprises all animated beings, has been revealed in its full extent:

52. 'Thus, by indulging the sensual appetites, and by neglecting the performance of duties, the basest of men, ignorant of sacred expiations, assume the basest forms.

53. 'What particular bodies the vital spirits enter in this world, and in consequence of what sins here committed, now hear at large and in order.

. . . .

81. 'With whatever disposition of mind a man shall perform in this life any act (religious or moral), in a future body endued with the same quality, shall he receive his retribution.

III.

HUMAN ORIGIN AND THE VEDIC REVELATION.

ॐ ब्रह्मा देवानां प्रथमः सम्बभूव विश्वस्य कर्त्ता भुवनस्य गोप्ता ।
स ब्रह्मविद्यां सर्व्वविद्याप्रतिष्ठामथर्व्वाय ज्येष्ठपुत्राय प्राह ॥ १ ॥

'AUM'! Brahmâ, the creator of the Universe and the preserver of the world, was the first produced amongst all the Gods. He taught the science of Brahma, the foundation of all sciences to his eldest son Atharva. Atharva Veda Mundaka Upanishad-First Mantra.

यत्तत्कारणमव्यक्तं नित्यं सदसदात्मकम् ।
तद्विसृष्टः स पुरुषो लोके ब्रह्मेति कीर्त्यते ॥ ११ ॥

He who is the (First) Cause, the Unmanifested (not existing as the object of our sense), the Eternal (without beginning or end), possessing the nature of reality (Absoluteness) and unreality (Illusiveness), produced the Divine Male known in all the worlds under the appellation of Brahmâ. Manu, First Chapter, śloka 11.

सर्वेषां तु स नामानि कर्माणि च पृथक् पृथक् ।
वेद शब्देभ्य एवादौ पृथक् संस्थाश्च निर्ममे ॥ २१ ॥

It was He who first assigned to all creatures distinct names, distinct acts and distinct occupations, as they had been revealed in the pre-existing Veda. Manu, First Chapter, śloka 21.

अग्निवायुरविभ्यस्तु त्रयं ब्रह्म सनातनम् ।
दुदोह यज्ञसिद्ध्यर्थमृग्यजुःसामलक्षणम् ॥ २३ ॥

From Fire, from Air, and from the Sun, Brahmâ milked out (as it were) the three primordial Vedas, named Rich, Yajush, and Sáman, for the due performance of the sacrifice. Manu, First Chapter, śloka 23.

TRADITION tells us that the human race has been procreated by a single pair (one man and one woman). This tradition is founded partly on religious books and partly on verbal information handed down from generation to generation. After all, this does not seem to be an idle theory. Adamites trace their generations back to Adam* and it is very easy for us, the Hindus of the present day (viz., the twice-born classes), to trace back our origin to Brahmâ, the first progenitor: because, if not all, at least a majority of the different sections of the upper three classes have a Gotra or a tribal name informing them of the first Man from whom the tribe has descended These progenitors, ten in number, were the sons of Manu who was produced by Brahmâ. (See Manu, Chapter First, śloka 34). But even now if we trace any tribe or nation back to its origin, we may arrive at the same result, namely, that there was a single pair at its origin, though this enquiry may lead us to far remote times of which the accounts may appear incredible at a first reading. To ascertain the truth of what has been stated above, one must go to a District Revenue office, where the geneological trees of the inhabitants of all the different villages in the District are kept, and he will, in a majority of cases, find that each of the tribe in the different villages is there traced to a single ancestor, and if the search were continued and all the information were forthcoming, which at the present day is perhaps impossible to procure, he will surely be able to trace the different tribes to one common

* The first progenitor of the human race Brahmâ or Prajâpati, is also called Adi-Manu or the first Manu of the first Manvantra. The western nations give the name of âdim (adam) to the first Manu and the name of Nuh (Noah) to the Manu who survives the deluge. The words are really the same as those of Sanskrit. The letter 'M' of Manu is wrongly affixed to the word Adi, making it Adim and Manu with the letters 'M,' 'A' omitted would be Nu or as the word is spelled Nuh. The descendants of Manu are called in Sanskrit Mânava, in Himalayan Mánoo, Saxon man.

ancestor in the same way as the different members of a family are traced to one ancestor and the different families of a tribe to a single progenitor. We have shown that there is a time when the evolution of the world takes place, and, as a consequence of the above argument, it necessarily follows that there must have been a common progenitor of the race at the beginning of human origin. We have already shown under the authority of Manu, Chapter XII, śloka 50, that the highest condition to which by the good quality a soul can be exalted is that of Brahmâ. As to how Brahmâ is born subjectively or potentially, one should study Manu on Creation, Chapters I and XII, Brihad Âranyaka Upanishad First Chapter, Fourth Brahman, with S'ri S'ankar Âchârya's commentary on the above, as well as on the first Mantra of Mundaka Upanishad. It is difficult for me to give here all the information necessary on the subject.

We know by experience that unless we teach our children they are unable to speak, and also that whatever knowledge we may teach them they will accept it as the gospel truth. The Great Akbar, the Mughal Emperor, once made an experiment as to whether children could learn to speak by instinct. He confined a number of children in a subterranean room and employed servants who were both deaf and dumb, and stored provisions for their support for some years; when the children grew up their utterances were found to be just like those of other animals. The human race is quite unable to learn any language or manners by instinct, and therefore if we suppose that the first progenitor was without any knowledge of language or manners it necessarily follows that different races must have remained as ignorant as was their first progenitor. But so far as religion and tradition go, we find that the first man was endowed with all knowledge, which he imparted to his offspring (see the quotations above). It is said that whatever Brahmâ taught to his sons was the pre-existing Veda or the Universal Knowledge of Science, philosophy and Religion. A child never feels any doubt as to the truth of the information his father gives him, nor do I know of a virtuous father ever misleading his children. It is absurd to believe that the first generations remained in the dark, and that revelation was only made when the world had grown wise enough to judge between right and wrong, and to condemn all who professed to be the agents of God for the purpose of communicating revelation to mankind as jugglers and imposters: to say that a revelation was made at a time when there was little or no need for it, is no wise theory. At the same time, if we believe that any particular person in a particular age was the only individual through whom revelation was destined to be communicated, a curious and surprising question arises as to the fate of those who had died before the advent of such a Medium or Mediator. But even if we take it for granted that a further revelation can take place when the human race has reached a certain stage of development, we must take into consideration the fact that revelation as a Divine help seems necessary only where human intellect fails to realize the true meaning of things. For instance, we find that ordinary Human intellect does not realize the existence of a Divine Principle, nor does it understand that the fruits of our present actions are to be reaped by us in our future incarnations. But I do not find any necessity for Divine help, in the way of revelation, in writing the history of a nation, or the biography of a person, which could be done by a man of average intellect. It may, therefore, be noted, that revealed books which contain more than three-fourths of past history, cannot under any circumstances be said to have possessed Divine origin; as it cannot be suppossed that God will help people in writing the past histories of men and nations. It is, therefore, necessary to believe that there must have been revelation at the beginning of human race, as believed by Vedic followers, and not after it. Hence our religious books teach us that in each cycle, at the beginning of human existence, there rises one who is called Prajâpati (Brahmâ), uniting in himself the qualities divine and human, as a fruit of the perfect and complete good actions performed by him in his previous incarnations. He is endowed with four innate transcendental qualities namely:—

(1) Unbounded knowledge (अप्रतिघं ज्ञानम्),

(2) Unbounded dispassion (अप्रतिघं वैराग्यम्),

(3) Unbounded power (अप्रतिघं ऐश्वर्यम्),

(4) Unbounded Righteousness (moral merit) (अप्रतिघं धर्म). This Prajâpati reveals the Vedas as learnt by him in the previous cycle of the world's existence. The knowledge of the Vedas thus imparted by Prajâpati, is called a revelation (re and Velum) the root meaning of which is a lifting of the Veil and thus an unveiling of what was previously veiled. The Vedas are therefore called Apaurusheya (not human composition) as distingiushed from 'Simriti' (what is remembered or what is the work of human origin), and the several sages to whom the hymns of the Vedas are ascribed, are therefore called (द्रष्टारः) 'Seers' and not (कर्तारः or स्रष्टारः) composers. The Vedas are also called 'S'ruti' (what is heard or revealed), because they were heard from Prajâpati who, in his turn, had heard them from others in his previous life. The word 'S'ruti' has also a deeper meaning attached to it, when the Adhyâtmic signification is taken ; it then establishes connection with Shabda Brahm and the Parà Vàni or the most subtle form of the voice of silence.

Thus a peculiar greatness is attached to Vedic revelation, namely, that the Vedas are handed down from one generation to another, in each cycle, as a divine inhiretance, and that they themselves bear testimony to this fact. For this we refer the reader to the following Mantras of Yajur Veda.

अन्यदेवाहुर्विद्याऽन्यदाहुरविद्यया ।
इति शुश्रुम धीराणां ये नस्तद्विचचक्षिरे ॥ १० ॥

They say that different is the effect of performing acts with knowledge and different is the effect of performing them in ignorance. This we heard from the sages who explained to us the effects of both (these actions), Yajur Veda, Chapter 40, Mantra 10.

अन्यदेवाहुः संभवादन्यदाहुरसंभवात् ।
इति शुश्रुम धीराणां ये नस्तद्विचचक्षिरे ॥ १३ ॥

They say that different is the effect of worshipping unmanifested nature; and different becomes the effect of worshipping that which has been manifested. This we heard from the sages who explained to us the effects of both (these worships). Yajur Veda, Chapter 40, Mantra 13.

IV

TEACHING OF THE VEDAS.

THE Vedas consist of two parts, *viz.*, Mantra Bhâga (Samhita) and Brâhmana Bhâga (including Upanishads)

Both of these are believed by orthodox Hindus to be Apaursheya, *i.e.* not written by man.

The Vedas treat of three topics, *viz.*,

(1). Karma Kânda (कर्मकाण्ड) Performance of good acts;

(2). Upâsanâ Kânda (उपासना काण्ड) Meditation; and

(3). Jnâna Kânda (ज्ञान काण्ड) knowledge of the Soul.

The part that particularly treats of the knowledge of the soul is called Upanishadas, and as it is always placed at the end of each of the Vedas it is called Vedânta, both because it comes at the end of the Vedas, and because it is the final object of their teachings.

The Karma Kânda and Upâsanâ Kânda were taught to all the twice born classes in the course of their study, and these they were enjoined to perform all through their lives until they acquired knowledge of the soul (Âtmâ) preached in the Upanishads. But the knowledge of Âtmâ was not taught by the sages (Rishis) till they found an 'Adhikâri,' *i.e.* a student fit to receive instruction on this difficult and intricate science. The sages used to test the ability of the student by making him undergo certain examinations and trials. He only was considered an 'Adhikâri' who had freed himself from sin (Mal) and unsteadiness of mind (Vikshepa), and who lacked only the knowledge of Âtmâ owing to the veil of ignorance (Âvarna) overhanging him. We will now describe the means by which one can free himself from 'Mal' and 'Vikshepa' (sin and unsteadiness) and thus become an Adhikâri.

V.

REMOVAL OF SIN OR IMPURITY.

मल (MAL.)

BEFORE considering the means as to the removal of sin, we should know what sin is and how it is incurred Manu's definition of the Juridical system is as follows:—"The roots of law are the whole Veda, the ordinance and moral practices of such as perfectly understand it, the immemorial customs of good men, and (in cases quite indifferent) self-satisfaction." (Chapter II, śloka 6).

" The scriptures, the Codes of Law, approved usage, and (in all indifferent cases) self-satisfaction, the wise have openly declared to be the quadruple description of the Juridical system" (Chapter II, śloka 12); and an act or omission contrary to the Juridical system is a sin.

In the article on re-incarnation of souls we have shown that when a physical act is performed, an impression is produced on the mind which transmits the impression to the deciding faculty Vijnâna and thence to the Conscious Soul. The impressions transferred to the Conscious Soul revert; and if the Vijnâna does not return them to the Conscious Soul, they travel to the mental circle which acts as an agent or instrument in the hands of Vijnâna (deciding faculty), and the action of this agent appears in the performance of bodily acts; the body being the place of manifestation of acts. The circle of mental powers is in itself blank but the impressions which it receives from the physical frame are transmitted by it to the circle of the Conscious Soul, and those received back from the latter, are transferred by it to the physical circle. If the circle of mental powers remains blank, one does not experience either pleasure or pain, but he becomes conscious of pleasure and pain only when the idea of pleasure or pain is present in the mind. We know by experience that when a man infringes the injunctions of his religion, the Codes of Law, approved usage, or self-satisfaction, he becomes apprehensive of the consequences of his act. The mind (Vijnâna) thus transmits a sinful impression or rather an idea of the expected consequences to the Conscious Soul. These impressions return to the mind, and when present therein, cause a peculiar motion which results in fear and dread. In proportion to the amount of sinfulness and frequency of infringement of the Juridical system, anxiety and fear remain present in the mind, and the deciding faculty loses, on account of the continued presence of fear and anxiety, its power of control, and is thus unable to give a proper decision on the merits of the impressions it receives. In other words, extraneous matter, consisting of fear and anxiety, is produced on the surface of the mental circle which covers its blankness. In Sanskrit 'Sin' is therefore called **Mal** (मल) or impurity, from its being the cause of such impressions as darken the mental circle.

Now the question is, how to remove this impurity. We know our own acts were the cause of this impurity, and so, evidently by our own acts again, we may purify the circle of our mind (Antahkarana), and make it once more clean. For a person to commit theft, adultery or murder is a sin, and although the sin thus incurred is not perceptible on any part of the body, yet one is nevertheless conscious of it. Thus, it is nothing more or less than an hostile idea present in the mind, and contrary to the law of harmony or any prescribed moral law laid down by any recognised authority. But the religion, usage, or law, which prescribes that the doing of an act contrary to it is a sin, also prescribes a mode for its expiation.

As the doing of an act contrary to the law of harmony has an effect of producing a stain on the mind, so an act in conformity with the said law of harmony has the effect of producing an impression of virtue and removing sin. Therefore, we say that by undergoing a punishment or performing a panance we become possessed of the idea that we are no more accountable for the sinful acts done by us. Thus there are two ways of ridding ourselves of sin ; (1) By undergoing penance or by expiation in the manner prescribed by the Juridical systems ; and (2) By counteraction, *i. e.* by performing acts of Virtue, and so possessing the mind with pure and virtuous thoughts as shall suppress the grosser sentiment, gaining the mastery over and stamping out all sinful impressions or intentions. Hence, Manu says :—" But men who have committed offences and have received from kings the punishment due to them, go pure to heaven and become as clean as those who have done well." Manu, Chapter VIII, śloka 318.

We give here the following ślokas from Manu, Chapter XI, on Penance and Expiation, in support of the foregoing theory.

44. 'Every man, who does not an act prescribed, or does an act forbidden, or is guilty of excess even in legal gratification of the senses, must perform an expiatory penance.'

45. 'Some of the learned consider an expiation is confined to involuntary sin only, but others, from the evidence of the Veda, hold it effectual even in the case of a voluntary offence:'

53. 'Thus, according to the diversity of actions, are born men despised by the good, stupid, dumb, blind, deaf, and deformed.'

54. 'Penance, therefore, must invariably be performed for the sake of expiation : since they, who have not expiated their sins, will again spring to birth with disgraceful marks.'

227. 'By these expiations are twice born men absolved, whose offences are publicly known, (and are mischievious by their example); but for sins not public, the assembly of priests must award them penances, with holy texts and oblations to fire.'

228. 'By open confession, by repentance, by devotion, and by reading the scripture, a sinner may be released from his guilt; or by almsgiving, in case of his inability to perform the other acts of religion.'

229. 'In proportion as a man, who has committed a sin shall truly and voluntarily confess it, so far he is disengaged from that offence, like a snake from his slough.'

230. 'And, in proportion as his heart sincerely loathes his evil deed, so far shall his vital spirit be freed from taint of it.'

231. 'If he commit sin, and actually repent, that sin shall be removed from him ; but if he merely say "I will sin thus no more" he can only be released by an actual abstinence from guilt.

232. 'Thus revolving in his mind the certainty of retribution in a future state, let him be constantly good in thoughts, words, and action.'

233. 'If he desire complete remission of any foul act which he has committed, either ignorantly or knowingly, let him beware of committing it again : for the second fault his penance must be doubled.'

234. 'If, having performed any expiation, he feel not a perfect satisfaction of conscience, let him repeat the same devout act, until his conscience be perfectly satisfied.'

235. 'All the bliss of deities and of men is declared by sages, who discern the sense of the Veda, to have in devotion its cause, in devotion its continuance, in devotion its fullness.'

242. 'Whatever sin has been concieved in the hearts of men, uttered in their speech, or committed in their bodily acts, they speedily burn it all away by devotion, if they preserve devotion as their best wealth.'

244. Even Brahmâ, lord of creatures, by devotion enacted this code of laws ; and the sages by devotion acquired a knowledge of the Vedas.'

247. 'As fire consumes in an instant with his bright flame the wood, that has been placed on it, thus, with the flame of knowledge, a Bra'hman, who understands the Veda, consumes all sin.'

248. 'Thus has been declared, according to law, the mode of atoning for open sins ; now learn the mode of obtaining absolution for secret offences.'

* * * * * * *

VI.

REMOVAL OF UNSTEADINESS OF MIND विक्षेपः (VIKSHEPA).

THE second obstacle to the attainment of spiritual knowledge is 'Vikshepa' or unsteadiness of mind. It arises from the uncontrolled state of the mind; for while we attempt to concentrate our attention on one object, the mind roams in different directions and becomes restless and unmanageable. As the reflection of the sun on the face of water throws back its trembling shadow on the wall, when moved by the waves of wind, so does the mind waver under the movement of its own Vrittis (or modifications of mind), going out and coming in through the doors of its five senses. The remedy for Vikshepa is found in the practice of Upâsnâ (meditation), of which a necessary ingredient is concentration of the mind.

Upásná means from its root (उप+आस+युच) sitting or drawing nearer and nearer to the object of meditation, till union is attained. Mr. Coleridge thus explains the meaning of the English word meditation, " For meditation is, I presume, that act of the mind by which it seeks within, either the law of the phenomena which it has contemplated without or semblances, symbols and analogies corresponsive to the same." From the above definition it appears necessary that the object of our meditation must be known to us. If it is unknown outside, it is impossible for us to meditate on it within. In order to perform the act of meditation, the image of our object of meditation must be so familiar to us that as soon as our eyes are shut, the mind should feel the image present, just as if it were seen with open eyes. But if the meditator has never seen the object of his meditation, it is absolutely necessary to have something before him representing the object on which he desires to meditate. This something representing the object, is called in Sanskrit Pratika (a symbol); and worship of this symbol is called Pratika Upâsnâ or symbolic worship. Now this Upâsnâ (meditation) is of two kinds, the inner or (Antaranga), and the outer or Bahiranga. To perform the inner Upâsnâ, it is necessary that the mind should be a cultivated one, and the meditator should have power to concentrate it inwardly on the desired symbol. Until the mind is so cultivated, it is necessary to make the outer Upâsnâ, the practice of which creates a power in the meditator to make the inner Upâsnâ. We keep pictures and images of our beloved friends and relatives in our houses, and, by looking at the picture, although it is only a representation of the original, we experience a pleasing satisfaction. This is the result of an act of outer meditation. Stories are also told as to how the ungovernable passion of love is created in certain minds by contemplating on the picture of some beauty, or even sometimes by simply hearing a description of the same. Idol-worship is therefore a mode of Bahiranga Upâsnâ. Some people, therefore, make an idol to represent the internal object of their devotion by an external symbol. The image thus made represents some individual qualities of the object meditated upon, as a picture represents the features of a person. For instance; Shiva is represented generally by a stone. Shiva, in Sanskrit means all-pervading peace or all-calmness, and is one of the names given to the Almighty God. The Rishis who taught Upâsnâ, finding, the mineral kingdom, of all others the one which possessed the greatest amount of calmness, and considering it the progenitor of all subsequent kingdoms of nature, selected a stone as the best symbol representing the All-calm Divinity. And, therefore, when Shiva is the object of our contemplation, we, for the purposes of our Bahiranga Upâsnâ, keep a stone before us. Idol worship, a misnomer for symbol worship, is one of the modes of Bahiranga Upásnâ, and leads to the attainment of higher spiritual knowledge. The highest and the most sacred Upâsnâ is that of Brahma whose symbol and natural name is Aum which altogether purifies the mind of Vikshepa, and, at the same time, helps to remove the veil of ingorance. Before stating the mode in which we should meditate on Aum, as laid down in the Upanishads, I think it is necessary to explain how Aum is said to be the symbol, as well as the natural name, of Brahma (The Great).

VII.

THE MONOSYLLABLE ओम् (Aum) ANALYSED.

IF it could be shown that all the different letters used to represent the elementary sounds of language, are contained in the letters of the Sanskrit syllable ओम् (Aum), written also as ओं (Aung), it can then be established, that if Brahma has any name formed of letters, that name is Aum. In making an enquiry as to whether all the letters of the Alphabets of the several languages are contained in this syllable or not, it is better at present to confine this enquiry to vowels only. The reason for doing this, is that the vowels stand to the consonants in the same relation as the soul to the body. As the body is dependent for its very existence on the soul, so the consonants depend for their very pronunciation on the vowels. Thus when we see that the consonants have no independent existence of their own, we will make an enquiry about them later on.*

---

* The Alphabet consists of letters which are marks or characters used to represent the elementary sounds of Language. These are divided into vowels and consonants.

In regard to these letters our assertion is, that the vowels have an independent sound of their own, while the consonants have not, and depend for their very pronunciation on the vowels. In support of this assertion we quote the following authorities.

स्वयं राजन्त इति स्वराः

In his Mahâbbâshya the Great Rishi Patanjli says—'A Vowel is that which shines by itself.'

अन्वग्भवति व्यञ्जनमिति

The same Maharishi says.—'A Consonant is that which cannot be pronounced without the help of a vowel.'

Mr. Hiley's definitions are :—"A Vowel is a letter that forms one continuous sound without interruption of the passage of breath."

"A Consonant makes only an imperfect sound of itself, as b, c, d, which cannot be distinctly articulated unless it is joined to a vowel."

The pronunciation of Aum in Sanskrit is, as of letters "Ome" in the English words "Home," "Rome" &c.

Let us now analyze the letters of which the word ओं (Aung) or ओम् (Aum) is a compound: these letters are अ (a) pronounced as 'a' in 'legal' and 'verbal,' उ (u) pronounced as 'u' in 'push' 'put' and म् (m) or 'anuswâra,' the nasal sound denoted either by the letter 'm' (म्) or the mark of a dot (.) at the top of the letters 'Au' joined together and written as ओं (Aung). This

---

Mr. J. D. Morell, M. A. LL. D., gives the following definitions :—

"The letters that have open sounds are called vowels (Latin Vocalis)."

"The consonants can be properly sounded only in conjunction with a vowel. They are therefore, termed consonants (Latin Con, together; Sonans, sounding)"

Webster's Dictionary :—

"A vowel is an utterance of the human voice made through a more open position of the organs than that with which a consonant is uttered. Consonant is an articulate sound which in utterance is usually combined and sounded with an open sound called a vowel."

Beeton's Dictionary of Universal Information :—

"Consonant (Con, and Sono I sound) in Grammar is a letter which cannot be sounded by itself without the aid of a vowel placed either before or after it."

Ogilvie's Dictionary :—

"Vowel—A sound uttered by simply opening the mouth or vocal organs; a sound uttered when the vocal organs are merely in an open position, as the sounds of a or o. Vowels are distinguished from consonants in that the former can be pronounced by themselves, while consonants require to be sounded with the aid of a vowel."

"When the voice is not further modified by contact, partial or complete, of the lips or tongue, but flows through an open channel without any friction or hissing, then we have *vowel* sound. When, on the other hand, the sound is not complete until the action of some part of the organs of the mouth has ceased, then we have produced what we may call *consonantal* sound. Briefly, a vowel is the result of an open position of the vocal organs; an articulation (this is Mr. Bell's term for consonant) is the result of an opening action of the organ."

PEILE.

"Vowels in all their varieties are really infinite in number. Yet, for practical purposes, certain typical vowels, each with a large margin for dialective variety have been fixed upon in all languages."

MAX MULLER.

mark of a dot called in Sanskrit Anuswâra is pronounced as English 'ng' is pronounced when forming the last syllable of a word, such as in 'song,' 'wrong,' &c. It

"Consonant, a letter, so named because it is considered as being sounded only in connection with a vowel. But some consonants have no sound even when united with a vowel, and others have a very imperfect sound. The consonants are better called *articulations*, as they are the names given to the several closings or junctions of the organs of speech, which precede and follow the openings of the organs with which the vowels are uttered. These closings are either perfect, and wholly intercept the voice, as in the syllables, ek, ep, et ; or imperfect, and admitting some slight sound, as in em, en. Hence some articulations are called mutes, and others semi-vowels or liquids. The consonants begin or end syllables, and their use is to determine the manner of beginning or ending the vocal sounds. These closings or configurations of the organs being various, serve to diversify the syllables, as in uttering ba, da, pa, or ab, ad, ap ; and although b and p may be considered as representing no sounds at all, yet they so modify the utterance of ab, ap or ba, pa, that the slight difference between these articulations may be perceived as far as the human voice can be distinctly heard. For distinction between vowel and consonant, see extract under Vowel."

We see that all these authorities agree on the point that consonants have no sound of their own, independent of vowels, and we cannot even think of their existence without their union with vowels. As consonants are always seen with vowels, we say that they are only a quality or a shadow of the vowels. But this cannot be said *mutatis mutandis* regarding vowels which have an independent existence, and do not in any way depend on consonants.

A real thing or entity is that which has an existence in itself, while that which has not a separate existence and depends for its existence on another, cannot be called a real thing or an entity.

Having seen that consonants have not an independent existence of their own, we cannot call them real things, but, at the same time, we cannot deny their existence because we are conscious of it. Their existence is therefore of a peculiar nature, which is neither real nor unreal. An only equivalent is to be found in the word quality or shadow. The quality is dependent for existence on some substance, and the shadow is an inseparable companion that attends a person or a thing. We never see a quality as apart from the qualified, or a shadow when there is neither any person nor thing present. It is, for this reason, that the enquiry has been confined here to vowels only, which are real as compared with the consonants.

For a further discussion on this point, see note to the 9th Shruti of ıe Mândukya Upanishad.

is now to be seen whether all the vowels of the alphabets of the several languages can be traced to the three letters of which the syllable Aum is composed. Sanskrit can, I believe, lay claim to possessing a larger number of vowels than any other language in the world. The vowels of this language may be enumerated as follows :—

(1) अ (A), (2) आ (Â), (3) इ (I), (4) ई (I′), (5) उ (U), (6) ऊ (U′), (7) ऋ (RI), (8) ॠ (RI′), (9) ऌ (LRI), (10) ॡ (LRI′), (11) ए (E) or (AI) (12) ऐ (AI′), (13) ओ (O or AU), (14) औ (OW), (15) the anuswâra (·) pronounced as "ng" at the end of a syllable and (16) visargani (:) pronounced as 'ah.' The last two are also called अयोगवाह : (Ayogvaha). For our present purpose, these vowels may be classified into three classes *viz.*,—

(1) (1) अ (2) आ (3) ए (4) ऐ (5) इ (6) ई (7) :
(1) A (2) Â (3)* E or AI (4)† AI′ (5)‡ I (6)§ I′ (7) AH.

(2). (8) उ (9) ऊ
(8) U (9) U′.

(3). (10) ओ (11) औ (12) ऋ (13) ॠ (14) ऌ
(10) O or AU (11) OW (12) RI (13) RI′ (14) LRI
(15) ॡ
(15) LRI′.

(4). (16) म् or (.)
(16) M or 'ng.'

The first of these is अ English 'A' pronounced as 'a' in legal, and verbal; and Arabic and Persian Alf (ا), and likewise Greek Alpha.

The second आ (Â) is only a long sound of अ (A) as 'a' is pronounced in 'alms,' 'art,' 'father,' &c.

The third letter is ए Roman (E) or (ai) which is a modification of the sound of the first letter अ (A), and its pronunciation in Sanskrit is like that of 'a' in 'ate' 'fate.' &c.

---

* Pronounced as A in Ate.
† " " A E in Aerial.
‡ " " I in Fit, Hit &c.
§ " " I in Idiom or ee in Fleet, Street.

Thus we know that the Sanskrit vowel ए is nothing more or less than अ with a modification of sound. The pronunciation of the English letter 'a' in 'ate' is a proof of this. In Persian this is written (اے), (Alf and Ye pronounced as ay), and this bears testimony to the fact that ए is only a modified sound of अ (A).

The fourth is only a long sound of ए (E) or (ai), and is pronounced just in the same way as the English letters 'a' and 'e' in the word 'aerial.'

We have just shown that this Sanskrit ऐ (AI') of which the English equivalent is found in the uninterrupted pronunciation of 'A,' and 'E' in the word 'aerial,' is only a long sound of ए (E) or (AI), and as the Sanskrit ए is nothing but the modified sound of अ (A), therefore its long sound ऐ (AI') is also a modified sound of अ (A) But we now find that the long ए *i.e.* ऐ (AI'), contains two distinct sounds, *viz.*, of long 'A' as in 'Ate' and of Roman 'I' pronounced as 'E' in 'Eton' The pronunciation of the Sanskrit ऐ ends with the sound of Sanskrit इ (I), and the clear inference that can be derived from the above analysis, is that the fifth letter इ * (I) is a part of the long sound of ए which, in its turn, is itself a modification of अ (A).

---

* In proof of this, we refer the reader to the Key to Pronounciation in the beginning of Webster's Dictionery where, in occasional sounds, the pronounciation of 'e' as 'a' short and 'a' long is given. Thus 'e' as short 'a' in ere, there, where, &c., 'e' as long 'a' in eight, prey, and obey. In his notes to para 11 of his Principles of Pronunciation, while discussing on the regular short sound of 'e' as in 'end,' 'met,' &c., Webster says: "This is not a short sound of the long 'e.' It has usually been considered as the shut or extreme short sound of the 'a' as in 'fate.'"

For a further discussion about the origin of the sound of इ (I) from अ (A), see Commentary on the 9th Shruti of the Mândukya Upanishad.

So far as my enquiry goes, the Sanskrit Grammar treats इ (I) as a separate vowel, but the 9th Shruti, in clear words, observes that अ (A) pervades in all the letters and there are several other Shrutis which positively affirm that अ (A) is the whole speech

Having shown that our fifth letter इ (Roman I) is only a modification of the first letter अ (A), it may be said that the sixth letter ई (I′) is only a long sound of इ (I), and is pronounced as 'e' in 'Eton,' 'evening,' 'east' &c. Now we have seen that letters 2 to 6 are only modified sounds of the first letter अ (A). It may be noted that the English vowel 'I,' as pronounced in First person Pronoun 'I,' is a compound of long 'A,' as 'a' in 'alms,' and long 'E,' as 'e' in 'Eton. The very pronunciation of the English letter 'I' shows that it is a compound of long 'A' and long 'E.' Otherwise its pronunciation is like that of short and long इ of Sanskrit.

The seventh letter is only a modified sound of अ, and is pronounced as 'AH.' It is, therefore, only अ (A) affixed to a short sound of the consonant ह or H. Here end the first seven vowels of our first class, and we find that these are all substantially अ (A) and the various modifications of अ (A).

Of the second class the 8th vowel is उ (U). Its pronunciation in Sanskrit is just the same as of 'U' in 'push,' or 'put.' The 9th is the long sound of उ (U) written ऊ and pronounced as 'oo' in 'moon,' 'noon,' 'soon,' &c.

The combination of अ (A) and उ (U) form the vowel ओ (O), which is the 10th vowel, class third. Its pronunciation is exactly as that of the English 'O' in 'old,' and the 11th Vowel औ (OW) is only a long sound of the 10th, and its pronunciation in Sanskrit is somewhat like that of the letters 'ow' in 'owl.' According to Sanskrit Grammar, we know that अ (A) and उ (U) combined make ओ ('AU' or 'O'). Thus we know that letters 10 and 11 are mere compounds of अ (A) and उ (U).

The 12th Vowel in the third class is ऋ (Ri) and the pronunciation of its Vowel Sound is different from that which the combination of the Consonant 'R' and the Vowel 'I' produces. For instance, the pronunciation of 'Ri' in 'Sprit,' is different from the pronunciation of 'Ri' in 'Spirit,' 'Merit,' but the Vowel

Sound of Sanskrit 'Ri' becomes 'A R' (अर) by rule of Âdesh (substitution) in the formation of words. The Vowel Ri (ऋ), of Sanskrit root Kri (कृ), becomes Kar (कर) in the formation of the word Kartâ (करता), from Sanskrit roots Kri (कृ) and Tri (तृ). The substitution always takes place between equals. As 'Ri' becomes 'Ar' by Rule of Substitution, it may be safely argued that 'Ri' is a compound of A and R. In other words, it may be said that Ri is a modified sound of अ (A). The 13th, is only a long sound of Ri.

The 14th Vowel is Lri (ऌ), and by rule of Substitution it becomes 'Al,' as in the formation of the word 'Kalpte' (कलपते), the root 'Klrip' (क्लृप) becomes 'Kalp'--It may as well be stated here, as already noted in the case of ' Ri,' that 'Lri' is also a compound of A and L. Hence it is argued that Lri is only a modified sound of अ (A). The 15th, is only a long sound of the 14th.

For a discussion on the letters RI and LRI (ऋ & ऌ) see Mahâbhâshya, First Adhyay, First Pâda, Âhnika IV, Sutra 9 and Kaiyat's note on the same ; as well as Dikshat's Sidhânt Kaumadi, Sixth Adhyay, First Pâda, Sutra 101, where it is said अकःसवर्णेदीर्घः

The 16th, is anuswâra, and its pronunciation is as that of 'M' in 'Bonum,' or of ' ng' in song, wrong &c.

Thus we see that the first seven letters are nothing but अ (A) or its modifications : the next two, Nos. 8 and 9, are only उ (U), and the third class, Nos. 10 to 15, are only compounds and really have no separate class of their own. The anuswâra is of the fourth class. We thus find that अ (A), उ (U).and anuswâra म् or (•) (M or 'ng') are the parents of all the other vowels in the Sanskrit alphabet. Of the English vowels, we have already treated of A,E and I, and there now remain O and U. We have shown that 'O,' pronounced as in 'old,' is equivalent to ओ, which is made up of अ+उ(A+U). The English vowel U as it is pronounced, is not a pure vowel ; it is made up of the Sanskrit consonant य (ya) and ऊ (oo). Leaving the consonant aside, we find oo ऊ in ' U.' In cases where 'Y' is pronounced as a vowel, it always sounds either as 'I' or 'E' and is therefore a further modification of 'A.' When 'W' takes the sound of a vowel, it is pronounced as the vowel preceeding or following it with the sound of 'A' or 'O.'

We have thus finished the English vowels, and find them all included in short 'A' (Sanskrit अ) and 'U' Sanskrit उ)

In Persian we have for vowels 'alf,' 'wao' and 'ye' (ی,و,ا) Persian alf is Sanskrit अ, and alf with 'hamza' (ء) is long आ (as 'a' in "father"). The Arabic ع (ain) is only double अ (a) (as in 'canaan'). The Persian 'و' (wao), when pronounced like (O), is a vowel, and when pronounced as ('wa') in واسطه '(wâste),' is not a vowel but a consonant; ی (ye) is a compound of य (ya), which is a consonant, and ए (E) or AĬ, which is a modification of अ (A)

The Arabic 'ء' (hamza) is nothing but अ with a short sound. We thus find that Arabic and Persian vowels are also absorbed in अ (A) and उ (U) of Sanskrit. In this way it can be shown that the elementary sounds of अ (A), उ (U) and म् or '·' (M or 'ng') are the roots of the Vowel sounds of the different articulate languages.

The doubt which may here arise as to the nature of the sound of anuswâra, is, that as letters 'ng' are both consonants, it may be said that the anuswâra is not a vowel but a compound consonant. To remove this doubt, we here quote what Dr. Noah Webster writes in para 83 while discussing the Principles of Pronounciation in the beginning of his Dictionary.

83. "The sound of *ng* (unmarked), as in *sing*, *singer*, *singly*, *&c*.

"*Note*.—This is a simple, elementary sound, and is not (as might be supposed) a compound sound made up of the sound of N in conjunction with that of G." . . . .

It may as well be stated that anuswâra, denoted by 'ng,' has got an independent Nasal sound, which may be pronounced even with lips closed. Here end the three letters of which the triliteral mono-syllable Aum is composed, and the analysis has shown that these three letters are the source of all the other vowels.

Grammar teaches us, as already shown, that consonants depend on vowels for their own pronunciation as well as in the formation of words, and it is for this reason that it has been said, that the life of all words are vowels. And it has now been seen by analysis that the number of all the vowels can be reduced only to अ, उ and '·' (A), (U), and (M or 'ng'). It follows, therefore, from the above reasoning, that these three letters are the life of all articulate words.

Now these three letters go to form the triliteral mono-syllable Sanskrit word ओम् (Aum), of the form of which we are fully acquainted with. We have a belief and are conscious that each of the letters, as well as the word formed thereby, has an existence. If these vowels had no existence, their compound could not be said to have any existence; for we know, that a non-existent thing cannot produce an existent thing. But we have before us the form of the syllable ओम् (Aum) or (Om), we see it written on paper, and hear its pronunciation and every body who sees it, who hears it, and, a blind man, who perceives its shape, says that he sees the syllable ओम् (Aum) written, or that he hears it pronounced, or that he feels its shape with his hand. Thus the conviction is that the syllable ओम् (Aum) exists as well as each of the letters अ, उ and म् of which it has been formed. This state of existence is called in Sanskrit (sat) Be-ness. This Be-ness we see in all the component letters as well as in the mono-syllable formed by them, but when we write ओम्, and pronounce it as Aum, we do not see or hear this Be-ness; the idea of this Be-ness, is simply present within our knowledge when we see or hear it. This abstract idea of Be-ness has no form or name, and is only realized by men of refined intellect. Hence it is said that the syllable 'Aum' is made up of four parts. Of these four, three are elementary sounds, to represent which we have made some forms or characters. These characters are called in Sanskrit Mâtrâs, that is, they are the standard of measure by which speech is measured (from Sanskrit root मिति to measure), or, in other words, they are signs or symbols of certain sounds, which really could be heard, but not seen. In order to remember again what has once been spoken of, we express the sounds we heard, by the symbols we had prescribed to express these sounds, and are thus in a position to know, by those symbols, the sounds once pronounced, but heard no more by the physical sense of hearing. Now we have Mâtrâs for the sounds of अ (A), उ (U) and '.' (M or 'ng'); but we have no Mâtrâ or even a sound, for that (sat) Be-ness, by reason of which each of the primitive self-dependent Mâtrâs (*i. e.* the said three letters) and their compound ओम् (Aum) are considered to be real and existing. Thus the three parts of the syllable Aum are represented by characters or symbols, and the fourth, which exists in all states, and which is the life of elementary letters and their compounds, has no Mâtrâ, that is to say, it is not signified by a character or a symbol, and is therefore called Amâtra (unmarked).

VIII.

THE UNIVERSE ANALYZED INTO PHENOMENA.

EXACTLY like the four component parts of the word Aum or Om (ओम्), the Universe before us also consists of four parts. The Universe is known to us only by its qualities, which may be described as follows :—

(1) Qualities perceived by the senses.

(2) Qualities conceived by the mind (whether in the wakeful or the dreamy state).

(3) Qualities still in a much subtler state, and therefore unknown to the mind.

The gross outwardly manifested world, perceived through the senses, is represented by the letter अ (A), the first mâtrâ of ओम् (Aum), as will be fully explained in the 'Mândukya Upanishad' hereafter.

The subtle manifestation, hidden from the senses, and conceived by the mind only, is represented by the letter उ (Ü), the second mâtrâ of ओम् (Aum).

The third is the unmanifested world, which constitutes the unknowable part, and which it is impossible to know before its manifestation, is represented by Anuswâra or म् (M), the third mâtrâ of ओम् (Aum).

We have seen the fourth or non-symbolic Be-ness in the mono-syllable ओम् (Aum), and we have now to find what equivalent there is to that Be-ness in connection with the material world before us. In the perception of the gross manifested world through the senses, the mind comes into contact with the grosser qualities of matter ; and where the instrumentality of the senses becomes powerless to help the mind in perceiving the finer qualities, the mind itself comes into contact with them, and, lastly, where the mind fails to grasp any of the qualities on account of their being in a much subtler state. Everybody should know that what the mind conceives or perceives, or which it is unable to conceive or perceive, of the material world, are only the qualities, and not the matter itself of which these are the qualities. The next generally admitted formula is, that the qualities have no independent existence of their own and exist only in some substance. Now we see that the qualities undergo change. They appear manifest (gross) at one time and become unmanifest (finer) at another. But the change always takes place in some substratum. It therefore follows that there is some substratum in which a change of the qualities takes place, and that this substratum is the entity, which is the holder as well as the sustainer of the qualities of the three descriptions noted above.

From the above hypothesis our inference is, that whatever of the outer world we perceive or conceive they are, in fact, the mere qualities of some substance and not the substance itself. The firm belief in the existence of this real substance or entity, of which the above-noted phenomena of three descriptions are qualities, is realized only by the help of supersensuous intelligence: although the entity itself is imperceptible and inconceivable ; and, in the words of Sir William Hamilton, "is conceived merely by a negation of conceivability." This entity is called the Self or Âtmâ of the ideal and material world. It is always manifested or expressed by qualities. Whatsoever we cognize in this world, and whatsoever we describe, are merely qualities. We can never define the real entity. The difference between a quality and an entity is, that the former undergoes change while the latter does not. This entity, devoid of all qualities, is Âtmâ or unqualified universal soul (Nirguna Brahma), and when known in conjunction with qualities, is called qualified universal soul (Saguna Brahma). This Âtmâ is the Fourth, and is equivalent to non-symbolic Be-ness of the mono-syllable Aum (ओम्).

Having arrived at the conclusion that Âtmâ is the underlying reality of all that is manifest and unmanifest, it may be said, from a Pantheist's point of view, that all that exists is Brahma. When Âtmâ is looked upon in conjunction with the three qualities noted above, it is the Source of all manifested and unmanifested qualities. In this sense alone Brahma is the cause, and the Universe its effect; as a piece of gold is the cause, and the different shapes of jewels made therefrom are its effects.

But following the principle that something is produced from something, and that it is impossible that non-existence may become the cause of existence, it may be truly asserted that whatsoever we see manifested in nature (effect), must have existed in qualified Brahma (the cause). Therefore, whatsoever we may find in the Universe, we ascribe to its cause.

The analysis of the Universe before us, shows that there are :—

(1) Things in the world which have got an existence, but which do not exhibit any external signs of vivid consciousness, such as minerals. The consciousness in the mineral kingdom, is in an extremely undeveloped state.

(2) Things that have got both an existence as well as partially developed state of consciousness, as the vegetable kingdom.

(3) Things which have got both an existence and a comparatively more developed state of consciousness, as observed in the animal kingdom.

(4) Things that have existence, and also a greatly developed state of consciousness, together with the enjoyment of blissfulness. The state of true blissfulness may be called that state, or condition of the human mind, in which a person, endowed with consciousness, cognizes nothing, but only blissfulness, as for instance in sound sleep or trance.

The first two classes demonstrate greatly the abstract quality of Be-ness (सत्). The third class shows a preponderance of Be-ness as well as Consciousness, or the animating principle (चित), and the fourth class shows at once the existence of Be-ness, Consciousness, and Blissfulness (आनन्द) all combined in one.

Having seen that the things in the Universe manifest the quality of Be-ness, consciousness and Blissfulness only, we jump at once to the conclusion that its first cause the Brahma, must necessarily consist of Be-ness (सत्), Consciousness (चित), and Blissfulness (आनन्द). It is therefore said that Brahma is an embodiment of सत् , चित, आनन्द (Be-ness, Consciousness and Blissfulness).

It may be noted here that the unqualified Âtmâ, the underlying Reality of the Universe, never undergoes any change whatever. The qualities, which depend for their existence on this reality, undergo various changes. To a superficial observer, the changes of qualities seem to be the changes of the Âtmâ itself, and he thinks that Âtmâ itself is undergoing a change, and it is to them (and not to the wise) that Âtmâ appears as inseparable from the different qualities.

IX.

CONSCIOUSNESS, THE CAUSE OF THE PHENOMINAL UNIVERSE.

BRAHMA, as defined in Chapter VIII, is the cause of the Universe, and is said to be an embodiment of Be-ness, Consciousness, and Blissfulness. This first cause is said to have expanded itself into multifarious effects.

But an action is always the result of volition, and volition is a quality of Consciousness. The result of this hypothesis, therefore, clearly is that by Consciousness alone was this manifestation made. Let us make a further enquiry into the subject as to how this Consciousness became the cause of manifestation. We know that the words which we speak, when heard by another, convey to the hearer the knowledge of the speaker, or, in other words, the knowledge of the particular state of things of which the speaker is conscious and which he desires to impart to the hearer; and the hearer, on becoming conscious of the knowledge which the speaker desired him to be acquainted with, bears testimony to the fact by saying, "yes, I understand you". A still further enquiry is necessary as to the words which, when uttered, become a vehicle for carrying the knowledge which it is desired to convey.

An utterence when made conveys with the sound a certain knowledge, but the sound is not in itself knowledge, because when the hearer hears the sound, he retains the knowledge which the words convey as apart from the sound of the words which conveyed it. Therefore, we say that words are the vehicle for conveying the knowledge. For instance, the hearing of certain articulations at once convinces the hearer that he who utters them is suffering pain, or is experiencing pleasure. This knowledge, which is retained, is something different from sound, the vibrations of which expand into larger and larger circles until they are apparently lost to the human ear. Thus it appears that the words expressed by sound, carry with them knowledge or consciousness, and it is for this reason that although articulate sounds called words which are mere vehicles for conveying knowledge are used to denote knowledge which is the real thing conveyed by them. The above allegory also appears in the Gospel of John the Apostle in Chapter I, verses 1—5.

(1) " In the beginning was the Word and the Word was with God, and the Word was God."

(2) " The same was in the beginning with God."

(3) " All things were made by him ; and without him was not anything made that was made."

(4) " In him was life ; and the life was the light of men."

(5) " And the light shineth in darkness ; and the darkness comprehended it not."

The unchangeable Âtmâ, void of qualities and conditions, is described only as the essence of I-am-ness (*i.e.* Be-ness). When Âtmâ, viewed superficially, appears as displaying qualities, it is known as Saguna Brahma (*i. e.* Qualified Divine Power). But when we think of the process of the Evolution of this world, we find that knowledge is the last thing to which the origin of this Universe is traced: this knowledge, or consciousness, belonging to the Universal Soul, is necessarily universal. It has already been shown that, figuratively the expression " Word " signifies knowledge or consciousness, hence John the Apostle rightly observed that in the beginning was Consciousness, and this Consciousness existed in Be-ness ; but when superficially observed, this Consciousness itself appeared as the Almighty God. To remove the doubt that Consciousness itself was not the reality, but only a quality, the second verse makes it more clear by saying that Conciousness existed in God. In the third verse it is said that all the manifestation was made by Consciousness only, and in the fourth verse that Consciousness is life and this Consciousness is the light of man. The fifth verse says that in the unmanifested state, commonly known as chaos or darkness, Consciousness shone as light, but darkness being unconscious, could not cognise the conscious being. The state of dreamless sleep is like the unmanifested state which existed before the Cosmic Evolution, and is defined as chaos or darkness and when we come out of this state, we express our consciousness of darkness, only. John the Apostle, therefore, said that the darkness, being in itself unconscious, knew not the conscious being that dwelt within its bosom.

It is quite reasonable for a man to enquire at this stage as to where existed all the various forms which we now find in the Universe before their manifestation took place, or, in other words, one may ask where existed the form of a table or a chair in a piece of wood before the table and chair were actually made. The reply in the last case is unhesitatingly given that the form existed in the knowledge of the carpenter, who is a conscious being. Therefore, all the different forms seen in Universe are said to emanate from the Divine Knowledge, or, in other words, everything that has an objective appearance has also a subjective model, this is called Ideation, and this Universe is formed after the Universal Ideation which always existed in the Divine Knowledge, or the Consciousness of the Ishwara. Things produced from knowledge must be of the same nature with their cause. Here knowledge is the cause of the forms, and it is manifested by means of gestures and sounds. The gestures and sounds thus become the vehicle of knowledge. It is evident, therefore, that when knowledge manifests itself in different forms, we do not find ourselves in want of expressing or signifying the same by means of signs or sounds. This shows that all the forms that manifest themselves at any stage must have already existed in knowledge. All the different discoveries of science and the appearance of new forms and shapes are not novelties at all. Everything existed already in knowledge. It is only a matter of succession or a question of time which causes the illusion of showing certain things as old and others as novelties, discoveries and inventions. The earlier phenomena, having become familiar to us, are known as old things, and the later ones, being previously unmanifested, are called new ones. In short, the whole Universe, with its different and countless forms and shapes that are either manifested or will hereafter be manifested, had its pre-existence in the knowledge of the Universal Conscious Being, Brahma. The forms when destroyed are not lost for ever. Their destruction only means their disappearance from the region of our senses and reversion to the source of their origin, *i. e.* the knowledge, where they remain till brought again into manifestation. The knowledge, therefore, is the source (Utpatti), the support (Sthiti), and the last resort (Nivritti) of all forms. It has now been shown how and why Brahma as an embodiment of consciousness, is considered and called the source or the cause of the Universe. As effects always exist in their cause, so likewise, the Universe exists in Brahma. As effects, when dissolved, disappear into their cause, so, likewise, the Universe, when dissolved, also reverts into its cause, Brahma. Therefore, Brahma is said to be the last resting place or the END—ALL of this phenominal Universe.

X.

AUMKÂRA IS THE NATURAL NAME OF GOD.

HAVING shown that there is a Being which manifests itself in the huge structure of this vast universe, and that that Being is known by the name of Brahma, we state that if this Being could be given a name, it must be such as should comprise within itself the infinite number of words that can be formed to denote the infinite number of things of this infinite universe. In other words, the name should correspond with the object named in possessing the three attributes of being at once the source, the support, and the last resting place of the words it begets. As the universe emanates from Brahma, so there must be a word from which all the words in the world emanated, and as the creation finds support and existence in the knowledge of Brahma, so also all other words must find their support in this one word, *i. e.* they must be dependent for their existence on that word, and as all the creation again disappears in its great cause, Brahma, so should all words be again dissolved into that word. But we have already seen that there is no word in the world existing independently of vowels, and we have seen that vowels, when analysed, are found to be only अ, उ and म् and that these three letters go to form the word Aum (ओम्). It may, therefore, be truly said that 'Aum,' the fountain-head of all the words, is the only word which can lay claim to be the real name of Brahma, the source of all manifestations. This word ओम् is the vehicle or body of universal knowledge, and is a natural name as described in the Upanishads and not a name given by mankind. By saying this we, at the same time, mean to say that it is the only name without a synonym. Names are of two sorts: (1) Unqualified or natural and (2) Qualified or characteristic. The name, irrespective of qualities, is called the natural or real name, and there is always only one real name originally given irrespective of qualities. It may, of course, be urged that men as well as things have often more than one name. But if we take any particular case and make an enquiry into the nature of those names, we will very soon come to the conclusion that there is one name and only one that is a real name, and the others have been subsequently given in consequence of certain characteristics. I think we may illustrate the philosophy of names by giving some examples. For instance, a child is given a name when it is only a few days or months old. Excepting some bodily features, it has then no other qualities, and, at the time of giving the name nobody knows what sort of man the child will turn out later on. A name founded on qualities changes with the qualities, but the real name never changes. Names are sometimes given to children based on personal features, or in connection with some occurrence at the time of birth But, whatever may be the case, the name first given becomes the real or natural name. Because, although at a later period, the features and circumstances on which the name was given change, the name originally given remains the same. Hence, we call this a real name. Take, for example, the case of a child who, having been born in poor circumstances, was given a name, say *gharibu* (pauper). He subsequently becomes a great man, say one of the wealthiest in the world, yet he will be called *gharibu* (or pauper). We find that another child is given the name of *Bâdshah* (king), and he is always called by that name, though by profession he turns out to be a fruit-seller only. The real name never changes, while we find that the names founded upon qualifications only change with the qualifications. For instance, the person who is now called 'Prince of Wales' will some day be called King of England. The same person in a regiment is first called a Subaltern or Lieutenant, then a Captain, a Major, a Colonel, and lastly, a General. Take the case of Jesus of Nazareth. His real name was Jesus, but the names founded on his qualities were 'Christ,' 'the Crucified,' 'the Lamb,' 'the Son of God,' 'the Saviour,' and so forth. Likewise, there are some hundreds of names given to S'ri Krishna of India. The real name is Jesus or Krishna, and the qualifying names are many. Therefore, when we say that 'Aum' is the natural name of God, we mean that this is a name irrespective of specific qualities, and when we say that Aum is the only name of Brahma, we mean to say that all other names given by the religionists or philosophers in the world are qualifying names, or names given by men to God, according to their own ideas, in reference to certain qualities.

Before explaining the sublime and sacred Philosophy, according to which the similarity of Aum with Brahma is shown in the Upanishads, we will dwell a little longer on the subject by expressing the grandeur and sublimity of this sacred name, as seen all around us in this world.

XI.

EVIDENCE OF SUBLIMITY OF THE MONOSYLLABLE AUM.

WE find that of the animal kingdom man is endowed with a developed faculty of speech, and the first articulations of a little child are no other than A (अ), U (उ) and the nasal sound denoted by *ng* or M. The child when it weeps, repeats the divine universal name, though uttered unintelligibly on account of its defective organs. For in weeping a child's voice is always heard as *úṇ*, *úṇ*, *úṇ*, or *aung* pronounced as a short sound. Children in their infancy have a tendency to speak, and those of the Hindus are taught to utter the word *úggúṇ*, or a corruption of Aung. The child first begins to say म or *Má.* When a child wants to point out a thing, it will say nothing but उ (U or OO). We again see that a man whose name we do not know responds when called by the sound of the vowel 'O'. If there is a crowd, and we address it by 'O,' the crowd becomes attentive to us, and the articulation 'O' is the common voice of exclamation with nearly all the nations in the world. When we address God, we address Him with the sound of the English letter O. There is a deep philosophy underlying the fact why in addressing God we only take the first two vowels अ and उ=ओ, and leave out the nasal sound. The reader will himself understand this when it is shown what qualities of Brahma are signified by each of the letters of the syllable 'Aum.' We will here give another instance. A man when very much distressed with some pain gives utterance to the long sound of '*húṇ*,' '*húṇ*,' repeated again and again for hours till he gets some relief. This '*húṇ*' is also spelled in English 'hum.' Dr. Webster says that, used as a verb, it means to murmur to drone, and as a noun, it signifies an inarticulate sound or murmur, uttered by a speaker in pauses from embarrassment. This *Húṇ* written in English *Hum*, is nothing but *úṇ* or *om*, spoken only with a slight modification, in order to make it expressive, that the speaker is in an embarrassed state, and implores mercy from his Creator by calling Him by His name. In India this sound of '*Húṇ*' is called, in common speech, '*Húṇga*', which is equivalent to '*úṇga*' or 'Aung,' the well-known epithet of Brahma. Likewise, expressions of pleasure and concurrence of opinion are expressed by the utterance of the English word 'hum' and Hindi *húṇ*, pronounced with a short sound, which is the corrupt form of the same Aum. The sound of laughter is a sound of many '*hums*' repeatedly made. Though sounds of laughter are also known as '*ah*' '*ah*,' repeated several times, with open mouth ending with many sounds of 'H', still the natural and common mode of laughing is the nasal and sonorous '*hum*' or '*húṇ*' spoken many times with closed mouth without interruption. Thus we see that mankind remembers the Great God by His real name, whether fully or partially uttered, at all times and occasions, both of pleasure and pain, and also on occasions when affirmation or concurrence is intended to be expressed. At the time when Sanskrit was a living language, the correct word Aum was always used on the occasions denoting affirmation.

It is a common saying in this country that a man remembers the Supreme Power in times of trouble, and here we have seen how far this saying is justified; and, at the same time, we see that the First Cause is remembered, not only in times of trouble and pain, but also in times of joy and mirth. As a natural result we see that whosoever hears the sound, whether he be a fellow countryman or a stranger to the tongue, manners and customs of the speaker, at once understands the motives of the speaker. If the sound is expressive of pain, he takes compassion, and if it expresses joy and mirth, the hearer partakes in it. It has been seen what wonderful effects the repetition of the full or partially expressed word *Aum* has. The expressions *ah*, *ha*, or *oh*, *ho*, or mere O, are partial names. The consonant in this enquiry is to be dropped, as it is used only to determine the articulation of a vowel, and what remains is either A or U or a compound of A and U equal to O. But if we make further enquiry into the question, we shall see that some animals and birds make utterances, the sounds of which correspond more or less with that of the monosyllable—ओं or ओम् (Aung or Aum). The cock, the pigeon and the dove, we find, end their calls clearly with, *úṇ* which is nothing but a modified and imperfect sound of Aum, as we have already shown. Likewise, we find that the bark of the dog ends with *Auṇ* and of most other animals with the nasal sound of '*ng*,' also pronounced in Sanskrit as M (म्). These are not things to be laughed at, but they rather require deep consideration. By making observations, the reader will find how far he realizes the truth of what has been said above. We again see that all music in the world is only a development of the nasal sound (Sanskrit 'Anaswâra' or म्). We know that all metals when struck give a nasal sound, the real and natural sound of Anaswâra, the English 'ng' or M. The science of music is nothing but a knowledge of different modifications of the nasal sound of 'ng'. The reader will find later on why we feel more delight in music than anything else, when he comes to know of the state of Brahma which this letter 'M' represents. Thus, we see that the natural name Aum is produced by all things in the universe in one way or another. In some places we see that the full word is pronounced, either correctly or corruptedly, whereas in other places one of its components only is pronounced, and in some the compounds formed by a combination of two of its letters are articulated. As each of the letters of (ओं) Aum is a representative of a particular state of Brahma, we find that the name of God is uttered everywhere either with all the qualities denoted by ओं or by some of the qualities denoted by each of its letters. It has been said that God, or the knowledge of God, is the cause or source out of which all things in the universe have sprung. We see that all things in the world have words to express them. We have also seen that Aum (ओं) is the name of the

Universal Spirit (Brahma), and that as the Divine Knowledge is the cause of all things, so the syllable Aum (ओं) is the source of all words. It may be stated, however, that as the different manifestations do not go to increase or decrease the merit or dignity of the Universal Spirit ; likewise, all the different innumerable words do not add to or lessen the value of the monosyllable Aum. Brahma and His name Aum, whether they exist as latent cause without objective manifestation, or when seen in the universe of effects, do not add to or lessen their own real value.

We will hereafter show, on the authority of the Upanishads, that Aum (ओं) is not only a name, but is also a symbol of Brahma. As the word Aum (ओं), has three parts, so also Brahma has three aspects. As the three parts (mâtrâs) of Aum are known by three different letters, so also Brahma is known to the world by its three aspects. As the fourth part, *viz.*, the Be-ness of the syllable Aum, is without a symbol, but exists in each of the mâtrâs (letters) as well as in the whole syllable, so Brahma, The Fourth, is the real entity, which was the substratum of the first three states, and is in itself without any qualifications:—good, bad, or indifferent. The Fourth, *i. e.* the unconditioned, is beyond the common understanding, and he who realizes his ownself, realizes it, *i. e.* the entity without qualifications. For instance, a person named Mr. John works as a carpenter, as an ironsmith and as a tailor ; when doing the work of a carpenter, he is called a carpenter ; when working as an ironsmith, he is called an ironsmith ; and when sewing clothes, he is called a tailor. The personality of Mr. John never changes with the change in his capacity. When seen as performing an act, he is then called an actor and is qualified by the character of the work performed, but when without work, he is not so qualified and is The Unconditioned. The conditioned Âtmâ in a human frame is known to us as qualified by three *states*, *viz.*, *wakeful*, *dreamy*, and *dreamless sleep*. In these three states it is named respectively as Vis'wan, Taijasan, and Prâjnan. The conditioned

Atmâ in the universe is called Brahma or the Universal Spirit, and also exists in three states, respectively called Virâta, Hiranyagarbha, and Ishvara. These are the different names of the conditioned Âtmâ viewed relatively, although the Âtmâ is always unconditioned, absolute and unchangeable. These three relative states of Âtmâ constitute the real trinity. On further observation, we find that in the universe all things, and in grammar all parts of speech, inherit this trinity from their parental trinity of Brahma and monosyllable Aum respectively. To show this heridity, we may here give a list, which, though very meagre in itself, is sufficient for our purpose to give some indication to the reader as regards the truth of the above statement.

TRINITY PERVADING THROUGHOUT THE UNIVERSE.

Universal Soul (Brahma)......	Virâta (Soul of the gross universe)	Hiranyagarbha (Soul of the subtle universe).	I'shvara (Soul of the unmanifested universe).
Human Soul	Viśva (wakeful).	Taijasa (sleepy).	Prâjna. (sound sleepy).
Hindu Trinity.....................	Brahmâ or Prajâpati, (The Created).	Vishnu (The Creator).	Shiva (The Holy).
Chiristian Trinity	Son.	Father.	Holy Ghost.
Prakriti (Nature)	Tamogun (Inertia).	Rajogun (Activity).	Satwagun (Lightness or goodness).
Crude Visible Matter	Solids.	Liquids.	Heat
Natural Creation	Mineral Kingdom.	Vegetable Kingdom.	Animal Kingdom.
Animal food consists of :—	Prithvi. (solids)	Jal. (liquids)	Agni. (heat)
Each of the components of this food, when digested, produces three things respectively.....................	Excreta. Flesh. Mind.	Urine. Blood. Vital air.	Bones. Marrow. Senses.
Stages of Life.....................	Childhood.	Youth.	Old Age.
Divisions of Body	Lower parts.	Middle parts.	Head.
Ranks of Life...	Low.	Middle.	High.
Actions	Bad.	Indifferent.	Good.
Result of Actions	Hell.	Earth.	Heaven.
Embarrassments	Adhiyâtmaka.*	Adhibhutaka.†	Adhidevaka.‡
Reality of things constitutes...	Name.	Form.	Action.
Things have	Beginning.	Middle.	End.

* Personal. † From other bodies. ‡ Supernatural.

TRINITY PERVADING THROUGHOUT THE UNIVERSE—*Contd.*

Divisions of day....................	Morning.	Noon.	Night.
The relative world consists of..	The objects of enjoyment.	The instrument of enjoyment.	The enjoyer.

TRINITY PERTAINING TO LANGUAGE.

Aum (ओम्)	अ (A).	उ (U).	म् or (·)('m' or 'ng').
The book revealed to Muhammad consists of	Alif (A).	Lam (L).	Mim (M).
Sounds	Short or extremely short.	Regular long or medium.	Extremely long.
Vedas employed in Yajna........	Rik.	Yajur.	Sáma.
Parts of Speech	Noun.	Verb.	Adjective.
Nouns have Persons	First.	Second.	Third.
,, ,, Numbers	Singular.	Dual.	Plural.
,, ,, Genders	Male.	Female.	Neuter.
,, ,, Cases	Nominative.	Possessive	Objective.
Verbs	Active.	Passive.	Neuter.
Tenses.....	Present.	Past.	Future.
Degrees of Adjectives	Positive.	Comparative.	Superlative.

XII.

MOHAMMADAN VIEW OF THE LETTERS OF WHICH ओम् (AUM) IS FORMED.

EVEN upto the present day, the respect for this invaluable name of God has not been lost among the professors of the Vedic religion. But it is a matter for regret that the other religionists, who once had an equal respect for this name, have altogether forgotten its value ; and although the Vedic truth is preserved in the books of their religions with great care, they do not understand it, nor do they try to do so.

Take, for instance, the religion of the followers of Mohammad. Their revealed book is Alkorân--Its first chapter is devoted to the praise of God only, and the subject matter of the book commences with the second chapter, the first verse of which begins as follows :—

الم ذالك الكتاب لاريب فيه

"A. L. M. This is the book, there is no doubt in it :" then follows a further praise of the book.

Before giving our own commentary on this verse, I would give the following extract from the Introduction to Sale's Translation of the Korân, and a translation in full of so much of the commentary on the Korân under publication, called Aksir-i-Âzam, as relates to the exposition of the letters A. L. M., with which the first verse of the second chapter begins.

Extract from Sale's Introduction (Page 42).

"There are twenty-nine chapters of the Korân, which have this peculiarity, that they begin with certain letters of the alphabet, some with a single one, others with more. These letters the Mohammedans believe to be the peculiar marks of the Korân, and to conceal several profound mysteries, the certain understanding of which, the more intelligent confess, has not been communicated to any mortal, their Prophet only excepted. Notwithstanding which, some will take the liberty of guessing at their meaning by that species of Cabbala called by the Jews Notarikon, and suppose the letters to stand for as many words expressing the names and attributes of God, his works, ordinances, and decrees; and therefore these mysterious letters, as well as the verses themselves, seen in the Korân to be called signs. Others explain the intent of these letters from their nature or organ, or else from their value in numbers, according to another species of the Jewish Cabbala called Gematria; the uncertainty of which conjectures sufficiently appears from their disagreement. Thus, for example, five chapters, one of which is the second, begin with these letters, 'A.' 'L.' 'M,' which some imagine to stand for *Allah latîf magîd*; God is gracious and to be glorified; or, *Anali minni*, to me and from me, *viz.*, belongs all perfection, and proceeds all good: or else for *Ana Allah Âlam*, I am the most wise God, taking the first letter to mark the beginning of the first word, the second the middle of the second word, and the third the last of the third word; or for *Allah*, Gabriel, Mahommad, the author, revealer, and preacher of the Korân. Others say that as the letter A belongs to the lower part of the throat, the first of the organs of speech; L to the palate, the middle organ; and M to the lips, which are the last organ; so these letters signify that God is the beginning, middle, and end, or ought to be praised in the beginning, middle, and end of all our words and actions: or, as the total value of those three letters in numbers is seventy-one, they signify that in the space of so many years, the religion preached in the Korân should be fully established. The conjecture of a learned Christian is at least as certain as any of the former who supposes these letters were set there by the amanuensis, for *Amar li Mohammad*, *i.e.* At the command of Mahommad, as the five letters prefixed to the nineteenth chapter seem to be there written by a Jewish scribe, Cob Yaas, *i.e.* Thus he commanded."

Translation of an extract from Ak'sir-i-Ázam.

In the name of God the most merciful, A.L.M. Tirmazi tells us by tradition from Abdulla, son of Masúd, that it has been said by the Prophet of God (peace be on him) that whosoover uttereth a letter of the Korân gains the reword of performing ten virtuous acts. I do not say that '*alif*' '*lám*' and '*mim*' written in Arabic is one letter, but *alif* is one letter, *lám* another, and *mim* a third. It is written in the Lamaát that even each of these letters (alif, lám and mim) is composed of three letters. Therefore, the uttering of the الم with which the chapter of the Korân known as 'Bakar' begins, earns (for the utterer) the reward of thirty virtues. These separate (uncombined) letters that occur at the beginning of most of the chapters of the Korân, have been recognized by most of the commentators as symbolic letters (Mut-shábihát), and the established and recognized view regarding them is that these involve mysteries of such a nature as are known to nobody but God and the Prophet. Abwal Sheikh and Iban Manzar have related by tradition, as follows, from Dáúd (David), who is stated to have said :—I asked *Shabi* to let me know the meaning of these letters. He replied, " O Dáúd (David)! Every book has some mystery, and the mystery of the Korân are these letters. Leave them alone, and ask anything else you like." The same has been related by Salabi and others, as tradition from Abubakar, Ali and others ; by Abdullais Samarkandi, as tradition from Umar, and Usman ; by Iban Masúd and Kartabi, as tradition from Savari, Rabi son of Khusaima, Ibn Anbâzi, Abu Hâtam and a class of traditionalists. Sakhâwi has written that it has been reported, as said by the *Sadar-i-awal* (*i.e.* the Prophet's companions and their contemporaries), that these alphabetical letters involve some mysteries which passed between God and the Prophet. We sometimes find some conversation taking place between particular persons in parables which others cannot understand. Another advantage of these letters is that they create a curiosity in the minds of those present to hear what follows them, and this is what was meant by the antiquarians when they said that these alphabetical letters have been put down to distinguish between the Faithful and the Infidels. This assertion is the truest one, but it leaves the doubt that, if these letters were such as conveyed no meaning, the Arab non-believers, before whom it was claimed that the Korân was written in a style unique in eloquence, and who failed to contest the claim, although they tried their best to find fault with it, would have directed their criticism and attack to this matter ; but they did not even express the least surprise at it. It is certain, therefore, that they *did* understand the meaning of these letters. Abubakar, son of Arabi, has written that if the Arabs did not understand the meaning of these letters, they would have been the first to bring this before the Prophet, because they were trying their best to find some fault in the Korân. But the chapters beginning 'Hâ' 'Mim' and 'Suâd' were read out to them, and they made no objection. On the contrary, they acknowledged the superior eloquence of its style. This is a reason for saying that this matter was well-known among them, which nobody could deny. We can conclude from these Arabic words that it is not strange if in the period of ignorance the orators of Arabia were in the habit of prefixing these disconnected or single letters (Mokattiât) to their sermons and lectures in order to show their eloquence. This admitted, there can be no other better explanation of these. But tradition does not prove it distinctly. It would be lengthy to state all the explanations given by the commentators, hence some only of the best will be given.

One authority says that these letters are names of God. This has been related by Iban Manzar, Iban Jurair, Iban Abi-Hâtam Iban Marduâ and Behaqi, by tradition from Iban-i-Abbâs. In his commentary, Iban-i-Mâja writes that it was said by Fâtima, the daughter of the Prophet and wife of Ali, that she heard Ali praying in this manner " 'O kâf,' 'hâ,' 'yâ,' 'ain' 'suâd—Forgive me." Some learned men interpret it by saying that he might have meant by this to say, "O sender of kâf,' 'hâ,' "yâ 'ain,' 'suâd,' forgive me." Another saying is, that these letters are names of the Korân. This has been related by Iban-i-Jurair, as a tradition from Majâhad, and by Abad, son of Hamid from Katâda. The reason given by them is that in many places the word *Kitâb* or *Korân* occurs so as to identify it with these letters, such as الم ذالك الكتاب (alif, lâm, mim, this is the book.) الم كتاب انزلناه Alif, lâm, mim, this is the book we sent) and wherever these single letters (Mokattiât) occur, they are followed by the word Kitâb, Korâu, or Zikar, or some other word of like meaning.

The third saying is, that these (letters) are names of chapters. This view has been held by many Mutkadamíns (a sect who profess to establish their religion by religious authorities and also by argument), Khalíl, and others. But the objection against this view is that there are no words from the Prophet, his companions, or their contemporaries, to support it. This, which is merely an expression of opinion by the moderns, cannot be believed, because chapters must have the same names which have been given them of old.

The fourth saying is that الم (alif, lám, mim) is nothing but the short of انا الله اعلم (ana allah aalam—God knows best). This has been related by Iban Abi Hâtam, as a tradition from Iban Abbâs.

The fifth saying is by Jauni, which is to the effect that these single letters (Mokattiât) have been used to serve as a warning. The reason is that the Korân being a book deserving great respect, it is necessary that it should be read out to a person who becomes attentive to listen to it from the very beginning, and, as the Prophet was in the habit of spending the greater part of his time in meditation and saying his prayers, it is possible that Gabriel was directed to utter these single letters (Mokattiât) to him, to draw his attention to enable him to hear attentively the words of God that were about to be communicated to him.

The sixth saying is that these alphabetical letters were mentioned to show, to the orators of Arabia, that the book (Korân) is composed of these very letters, in the use and employment of which they possess such mastery and control, but still they are unable to write in such a style. This is the view recognized by the Mobarrad and a class of enquirers (Mohakikin).

The seventh saying is that these letters have been used for the purpose of separating the chapters. Ahmad, the son of Yáhyâ, says, that the people of Arabia. when one subject ended and another began, were in the habit of using some such letters as had no connection at all with the subject that ended or the one that began. This was done in order to warn, the hearers of the commencement of a new subject.

The eighth saying is that God has sworn by these letters meaning thereby (as if God said) I swear by *alif, làm* and *mim*, that this is the very book which is written on the guarded table, (لوح محفوظ) on which, according to Mohammedans, the destiny of the Universe is recorded. The reason why he swore by these alphabetical letters is that they posses the honor of being the components of the words of God, his names and the words of his knowledge and unity ; and the words which man utters are also composed of these very letters ; and, although only some are mentioned, yet they purport to mean all letters."

XIII.

RECONCILIATION OF THE LETTERS A. L. M. OF THE KORAN AND OF THE NAMES OF GOD IN HEBREW, PARSI AND BUDHIST RELIGIONS WITH THE SANSKRIT A. U. M. (OM)

THE extracts given in the preceding Chapter show the great respect which the Mohammedan commentators of the Korân have for these letters. They believed these letters to be symbols signifying either the name of God or of his word (believed by them to be the Korân). I would particularly draw the attention of the reader to the 8th exposition of these letters, as given in Aksír-i Âzam. The commentator says that God swore that Alif, Lâm, Mim, (A. L. M.) is the very book which is written on the guarded table (Loh-i-Mahfuz), meaning unmanifested nature, and God says that 'A.' 'L.' 'M.' is the only book that existed in unmanifested nature. That which now appears to us is the manifestation of the same A. L. M. This exposition is just in accordance with the Philosophy of the Upanishads.

We are now to see whether these letters are the same or are different from those which go to form the syllable (ओं or ओम्) Aum.

In A. L. M., the mysterious letters of the Korân noted above, alif (A) and Mim (M) are the same as the Sanskrit अ (A) and म (M). The Lam (L) is used for the Sanskrit उ (U). The Arabic 'L' has sometimes a sound of 'U' when preceded by 'Alif,' as, for instance, 'Karam-al-din' is pronounced as Karam-ud-din. To make the mystery more mysterious, the letter 'L' has been used for 'U.' But there is no doubt that at the time when the Korân was written, the people of Arabia knew what these letters signified. Had it not been so, there might have been a good deal of critcism as to their use, and we should not have been able to get all the comments on the exposition of these letters that we now have.

Among the Western nations, the most ancient revelation is that of Moses, where it is stated that the Supreme Being revealed himself to the Jews by the appellation of Jehovah (Hebrew Hawah, to be), and this word signifies the sacred unpronounceable name of the Eternal, usually interpreted as signifying self-derived and permanent existence. The Jehovists maintain that the vowel points annexed to the word Jehovah in Hebrew, are the proper vowels of the word, and express the true pronunciation (Webster). The Jehovists are opposed to the Adonists who hold that the points annexed to the word Jehovah are the vowels of the word Adonai. Thus we find that, in the time af Moses, the vowel points of Jehovah, viz., E, A and O, or rather A and U, and their pronunciation as 'O,' formed of A and U, was the sacred name of God. While the Adonists believed before Moses that the name of God was 'Adonai' and that Moses only borrowed the vowel points of 'Adonai' to form the word Jehovah. In 'Adonai' we find the vowels 'A' and 'U' and also the nasal sound 'N'. The reader will see what great evidence we have among Westerns to prove that there is a very old idea that the most sacred name of God is formed by the letters 'A' 'U', or 'A' 'U' with the nasal sound. Mahommad recognized the revelation of Old Bible to Moses and up to this day, the professors of the religion of Moses believe that the vowel points of Jehovah denote the true pronunciation of the name of God, and hence it is quite reasonable to conclude that, at the time of Mahommad, the pronunciation of certain letters was considered to signify the most sacred name of God, and it is for this reason that some of the chapters of the Korân begin with the letters A. L. M., as signifying the name of God and denote the book revealed to Mahommad. All the Mahommadan traditions bear testimony to this interpretation.

The most sacred name for God in the religion of the *Pârsis*, the ancient residents of Persia, in the Zend language, is Ahurmuzd Yazdan. 'Ahurmuzd' is the principal name, and is formed of the vowels 'A' 'U' and 'M', which are exactly similar to those in Sanskrit.

The most sacred motto of the Lâmâs, the high priests of the Thibetans, Chinese, and upper hills of Northern India, is 'Aum Mâni Padmi Hom'. It is not surprising to find the syllable Aum in this motto, for the Buddhist religion was founded on the tenets of the Vedic religion of ancient India. The Vedas, in our present manifestation of the world, were handed down to us by Prajâpati.

The Prajâpati does not profess to be the author, but only the revealer of the Vedas, and therefore, there can be nobody to contradict the saying of the first man. In the Vedas, the letters अ (A), उ (U) and (˙) or म् ('ng' or 'M'), are considered to be the most sacred, and their compound the only name of God. The Vedic religion, being the first, the other religions must be considered as having sprung from it. History tells us that the division of the religion of a nation into various sects is the result of Time and Emigration. At the time of emigration, it is natural for all the offshoot-families to take the religion of the parent tribe with them; accordingly all the emigrating families took along with them the sacred name Aum. The difference that has sprung up in the pronunciation of the word is only due to the distance to which the offshoots emigrated. The people who continued to live in India preserved as much of the Vedas as they could, and preserved intact the word Aum formed of the elementary letters, while the offshoots, after a lapse of time, began to pronounce the same vowels with the union of consonants in one form or other. By and by, they forgot the sanctity due to the sacred letters, but still in the formation of all the names of God, the same vowels are continued to be used by them.

XIV

RELIGIOUS EVIDENCE AS TO THE SANCTITY OF THE MONOSYLLABLE AUM.

THE foregoing are some of the reasone as to why Brahma (the Great God) is known in the Vedic literature by the triliteral monosyllable Aum (ओम्).

The following extracts will show with what respect and esteem the word ओम् was adored by the ancients :—

MANU, CHAPTER 2, S'LOKAS 74 TO 85.

74. " A Brâhman, beginning and ending a lecture on the Veda, must always pronounce to himself the syllable Aum ; for, unless the syllable Aum precede, his learning will slip away from him ; and, unless it follow, nothing will be long retained."

75. " If he has sitten on culms of (Cusa) grass with their points towards the east, and be purified by (rubbing) that holy grass on both his hands, and be further prepared by three suppressions of breath, (each equal in time to five short vowels), he then may fitly pronounce Aum."

76. " Brahmâ milked out, (as it were) from the three Vedas, the letter A, the letter U, and the letter M, (which form, by their coalition, the triliteral monosyllable), together with three mysterious words. Bhu, Bhavah, Swah, or Earth, Atmosphere, Heaven."

77. " From the three Vedas also the Lord of Creatures, incomprehensively exalted, successively milked out three measures of that ineffable text, beginning with the word *tad*, and entitled Sâvitrî or Gâyatrî."

78. " A priest, who shall know the Veda, and shall pronounce to himself, both morning and evening, that syllable,

and that holy text preceded by the three words, shall attain the sanctity which the Veda confers ;"

79. "And a twice-born man, who shall a thousand times repeat those three (or Aum, the Viyâhritis, and the Gâyatrî,) apart (from the multitude), shall be released in a month from a great offence, as snake from his slough."

80. "The priest, the soldier, and the merchant, who shall neglect this mysterious text, and fail to perform in due season his peculiar acts of piety, shall meet with contempt among the virtuous."

81. "The three great immutable words, preceded by the triliteral syllable, and (followed by) the Gâyatrí, which consists of three measures, must be considered as the mouth (or principal part) of the Veda."

82. "Whoever shall repeat, day by day for three years, without negligence, that sacred text shall (hereafter) approach the divine essence, move as freely as air, and assume an ethereal form."

83. "The triliteral monosyllable is (an emblem of) the supreme; the suppressions of breath (with a mind fixed on God), are the highest devotion; but nothing is more exalted than the Gâyatrì: A declaration of truth is more excellent than silence."

84. "All rites ordained in the Veda, oblations to fire, and soleman sacrifices, pass away; but that, which passes not away, is declared to be the syllable Aum, thence called Akshara; since it is a *symbol* of God, the Lord of created beings."

85. "The act of repeating his Holy Name is ten times better than the appointed sacrifice; a hundred times better, when it is heard by no man; and a thousand times better, when it is purely mental:"

CHAPTER 6, S'LOKAS 69 TO 71.

69. "Let a Sannyási, by way of expiation for (the death of

those creatures, which he may have destroyed unknowingly by day or by night, make six suppressions of his breath, having duly bathed:"

70. "Even three suppressions of breath made according to the divine rule, accompanied with the triverbal phrase (Bhu, Bhavah, Swah), and the triliteral syllable (Aum), may be considered as the highest devotion of a Brâhman."

71. "For as the dross and impurities of metallic ores are consumed by fire, thus are sinful acts of the human organs consumed by suppressions of the breath, (while the mystic words, and the measures of the Gâyatrí are revolved in the mind)."

S'ri Krishna, in Chapter VII, S'loka 8 of his Bhagwat Gîtâ says, "I am the *Aum* in all the *Vedas*."

Further on in Chapter VIII, S'lokas 11 to 13 run as follows :—

11. "I will tell thee in brief about that seat which persons conversant with the Vedas declare to be indestructible, which is entered by ascetics freed from all longings, and in expectation of which people practise the vows of Brahmchârins."

12 & 13. "Casting off (this) body, he who departeth, stopping up all the doors (organs of sense), confining the mind within the heart, placing his own life-breath called Práua in the head, resting on continued meditation, uttering this one syllable Aum, which is Brahman, and for the while continues thinking of me, attaineth to the highest goal."

Among the Hindus, in performing a Yajna, the symbol ओम् is delineated at one corner of the altar, and is worshipped by repeating the following S'loka:—

ओङ्कारंबिन्दुसंयुक्तं नित्यं ध्यायन्ति योगिनः।
कामदं मोक्षदं चैव ओङ्काराय नमोनमः ॥

"The Yogins always meditate upon Aumkâra which has an

anaswâra (denoted by a point) on it. This Aumkâra is the bestower of all desires and salvation ; we bow down to the Supreme Aumkâra."

All the Purâns, S'âstras and Smritis adore the sacred syllable Aum ; and if extracts were given from all of them it would make a volume in itself ; we therefore stop here thinking that the quotations given above are sufficient to explain the views of the Smritis in regard to the sanctity of this sacred Syllable. Few more extracts will however be given from the Vedic Literature (Upanishads) at the end of Part II of this book.

PART II.

THE MÂNDUKYA UPANISHAD
OF THE ATHARVA VEDA

WITH

TRANSLATION

AND

COMMENTARY.

I.

HAVING shown that the syllable *Aum*, is the source of all words and articulations, as Brahma is that of the Universe, and also that *Aum* is the real name of Brahma, and not a name founded on attributes, we will now show how it is said that *Aum* is not merely a name, but also the symbolical representation of Brahma. The Mândukya Upanishad of the Atharva Veda treats only of the symbolic nature of this mysterious monosyllable *Aum*. It shows that each of its component letters is a symbol of each of the aspects, in which Brahma is known. The full word *Aum* is the full symbol of Brahma. The way of meditating on Brahma in each of its aspects is clearly laid down in the Upanishad above mentioned, and also how the meditator, by knowing the true nature of Brahma, and realizing the same in himself, obtains final beatitude ; we, therefore, give here a translation of this Upanishad with full and copious explanatory notes thereon, so as to enable the reader to understand its meaning.

MÂNDUKYA UPANISHAD

ओमित्येतदक्षरमिदꣳ सर्व्वं तस्योपव्याख्यानं भूतं भवद्भविष्यतिति सर्वमोङ्कार एव । यच्चान्यत्त्रिकालातीतं तदप्योङ्कार एव ॥ १ ॥

S'RUTI (1).

"Aum"—this syllable is all that is. Its explanation :—What was, what is, and what will be, all is verily Aumkâra. Everything else, which is not subject to the three-fold time, is also verily Aumkâra

NOTE.

The word 'Aum,' with which the S'ruti begins, is used as a name. It has been already fully explained in Part I., that the monosyllable 'Aum' is the only name of 'Brahma' the Universal Spirit. Grammar and language tell us, that the name of a thing or person denotes the thing or person, of which it is the name, as if *name* were a symbol or representative of the person or thing named. The words 'Jesus' or 'Krishna,' which are names of certain personages, who lived at certain periods of time, are respectively the symbols of the said personages. A picture of a thing or person, is to all intents and purposes, a symbol of the thing or person, which it represents ; but the name of the thing or person is a far more comprehensive symbol. On seeing a picture we describe it by naming the thing or person of which it is the picture. It follows then that a name is more comprehensive than a picture. In this S'ruti, the syllable 'Aum,' therefore, denotes the all-pervading Divine Essence (Brahma), of which it is a name. The Sanskrit word (Akshara) means from its root "that which does not decay or decompose." It, therefore, means immortal, and is an epithet of the Supreme soul. It also means a letter of the alphabet, अक्षराणामकारोस्मि amongst all the letters, I am the letter 'a' (अ). (Bhagvad Gîtâ, Chapter 10, S'loka 33)—it also means a syllable (Manu Smriti, Chapter 2, S'loka 83), the monosyllable एकाक्षरं (Bhagwad Gitâ, Chapter 10, S'loka 25 ; Manu Smriti, Chapter 2, S'lokas 78, 84, and 125), meaning the sacred syllable 'Aum.' Hence it means a word or words, or speech collectively. In translating the expression ओमित्येतदक्षरं as "Aum—this syllable," I have very correctly followed the commentary of S'ri S'ankarâcharya on Mândukya Upanishad. The word 'Aum' it will be seen, is put under quotation by the word इति (iti), (i.e. this) immediately following it. If the word 'Akshara' had been used to signify immortal (*i.e.* the Supreme Spirit), the use of the word इति (iti) and एतद् (etad) (meaning this) becomes redundant. But it is an established fact that brevity is the motto of the Upanishads, and a redundant word will never be found used in any of them. The word Akshara, as used here, therefore, clearly means the syllable 'Aum.' This very Upanishad also shows that this is the correct rendering of its meaning, as it shows in what high estimation and veneration the syllable 'Aum' is held by proving that *It* is a representative or a symbol of Brahma. The first sentence " Aum—this syllable—is all that is," therefore very clearly means that the Universal Spirit denoted by the syllable *Aum* is this *all*. In other words, all that exists in the Universe is the Universal Spirit denoted by 'Aum.' "Its explanation" ; S'ri S'ankarâcharya explains this sentence by saying that, as this syllable 'Aum' is the means by which the immortal being denoted by it is realized, its explanation 'should, therefore, be known.' But I think (as also does Ânandgiri) that the first sentence, *viz.*, "Aum this syllable is all that is," is given as an aphorism, asserting a problem, and then the S'ruti itself goes on to elucidate it, by saying that *the following is* its explanation. (The words in Italics being understood). The above exposition is supported by the rest of the S'ruti itself, which consists of an explanation of the first sentence. It says that all that is subject to three-fold time (manifest), and that which is beyond it (unmanifest), is verily the entity herein named as Aumkâra.

सर्वं ह्येतद् ब्रह्मायमात्मा ब्रह्म सोऽयमात्मा चतुष्पात् ॥ २ ॥

S'RUTI (2).

Surely all this is Brahma. This Âtmâ (self) is Brahma and this Âtmâ has (metaphorically speaking) four conditions* (Pa'das)

NOTE.

The word 'All' has been defined in the first S'ruti as meaning all that is subject to time, and other than that which is not subject to time. In other words, the word 'All' encompasses all the objective, subjective, and unmanifest world, as it exists in the Divine Essence. The first sentence, therefore,

---

* The Sanskrit word Pâda, literally meaning foot, is translated here as condition.

means that, undoubtedly, the manifest and the unmanifest world, comprised in the word 'All,' is Brahma. In the first S'ruti it is stated that 'Aum is all that is,' and in this S'ruti it is said, that 'Brahma is this all The conclusion, therefore, is that Aum is Brahma.

The next sentence is, 'This Âtmâ is Brahma.' The word 'this' एयम् (*Eyam*,) qualifying Âtmâ (Self), signifies something very near, as if the author points with his fore-finger to the region of the heart itself. The word Âtmâ means that which pervades all. A human soul is colled Jivâtmâ, as it pervades the whole of the human body. The all-pervading Divine Essence is called Parmâtmâ, as it pervades the Universe. The Âtmâ or spirit of a thing is that, on which the thing which is manifest depends for its existence. Now when it is said that this Âtmâ (pointing to the human Self) is Brahma, the author very clearly means to say (by inference) that the human Self, existing on the mundane body, is Aum, and the same spirit when pervading the Universe is called Brahma.

The next sentence of this S'ruti makes the problem of unity of Âtmâ (Self) with Brahma (the omnipresent spirit) still more clear, by using the word Âtmâ only in the sentence. "This Âtmâ (one's own Self) has four conditions." In Sanskrit Jivâtmâ is called the Individual soul, and Parmâtmâ Universal Soul. If, therefore, we deprive the Âtmâ of its qualifying terms, limiting it to an individual body or to the Universe, there remains the pure Âtmâ, which is the Self of all that is manifest and all that is not manifest. This is not our own idea of the words *All*, *Âtmâ*, and *Brahma*, but we see it in the clear words of the Divine Author as translated above. He says that all is Brahma; he then says that this Âtmâ is Brahma, and the natural conclusion is that all that exists is Âtmâ. This Âtmâ, the Self of all the manifested and unmanifested nature, is then described metaphorically as having four conditions or, more literally, feet. In reality there are three conditions only, and the fourth is the entity appearing in the three conditions. The first condition is described as follows :—

जागरितस्थानो बहिःप्रज्ञः सप्ताङ्ग एकोनविंशतिमुखः स्थूलभुग्वैश्वानरः प्रथमः पादः ॥ ३ ॥

S'RUTI (3).

The first condition is Vaishvânara, whose place is the waking State, who is cognizant of the external objects, who has seven members and nineteen mouths, and who enjoys the gross objects.

NOTE.

The first two S'rutis have shown the unity of Âtmâ with Brahma. The present S'ruti asserts, as established by other Upanishads, the maxim, that a man is a microcosm of the great macrocosm. The common saying equivalent to this in our contry is '*Joi pinde soi Brahmande,*' meaning thereby that whatsoever exists in one's own body also surely exists in the Universe. In other words, it means that human soul is the epitome of the Universal Soul, and human body is an epitome of the manifest Universe (which is itself the body of the Universal Soul). From the above it follows that the body of the Universal Soul must metaphorically possess all the members and organs possessed by the human body ; the only difference being that those of the former will be on a macrocosmic scale (Adhidaivaka), while those of the latter will be on a microcosmic scale (Adhyâtmika).

It will be useful to note here that this Upanishad is intended to show that the word Aum is the representative or symbol of Âtmâ, and as the word Aum has four parts (Mâtrâs) so Âtmâ has four conditions (Pâdas). These conditions, as enumerated further on in the Upanishad are, (1) The wakeful, (2) The dreamy and (3) The slumbering state. When Atmâ appears in the above states he is called respectively Vishvan, Taijasan, and Prâjnan. When it exists in its real nature, independent of conditions, it is called Turya, "The Fourth."

The Universal Spirit (Brahma), conditioned as above, is respectively called Vaishvânara, Hiranyagarbha, I'shvara, and Turya or Shudha Brahma. The above information is given here that the reader may notice that, in describing the conditions of Âtmâ, the author sometimes uses the qualifying names applicable only to the human soul, and the human body ; while at other times, those that are applicable to the Universal Spirit and the Universe: thus shewing that the distinction is only a nominal and not a real one. In order to enable himself to understand well the meaning of this S'ruti, the reader is requested to picture to himself the whole of the Universe as forming a human body on a macrocosmic scale. This body is described as having the following seven metaphorical members :

(1). The higher luminous worlds are compared to the upper part of the head, which contains the brain.

(2). The sun and the moon are the two eyes.

(3). The heat is the mouth.

(4). The directions of space are the ears.

(5). The atmosphere is (meant for) the lungs.

(6). The superterrestrial space (Antariksha *i.e.* the space between the luminous worlds and the earth) is the stomach.

(7). The earth is the feet (the emblem of the lower body).

These seven members of the body of Vaishvânara or Virâta, bear exactly the same relation to each other and perform the same functions, as these members are seen to have and to perform in the human body. As the Jivâtmâ (human soul) in its wakeful state* enjoys the external (gross) things by nineteen organs, rhetorically spoken in the S'ruti as mouths, likewise the Vaishvânara (Universal Spirit) in the manifest

* The Human soul in this state is called in Sanskrit Vishvan.

condition enjoys the gross material world by nineteen mouths or organs. These organs in a human body are as follows:

(1—5). The five organs of sense *viz.*, sound, touch, colour, taste and smell.

(6—10). The five organs of action *viz.*, the mouth the hands, the feet, the generative and the excretive organs.

(11—15). The five Vital airs *viz.*, (1). The air drawn in as by the act of inspiration, (2) The air expelled, as by the act of expiration, (3) The Equalising air, essential to digestion, (4) the circulating air, diffused through the whole body, and (5) the ascending air, which leads the conscious soul after death to a re-incarnate state.

(16). Manas (Mind).

(17). Buddhi (Intellect).

(18). Chitta (the faculty by the help of which things are recollected).

(19). Ahankâra (egotism or I-am-ness).

As the manifest Universe is a body of the Vaishvânara on Macrocosmic plane, so the nineteen organs of the living world in the Universe combine to form the nineteen organs of the Vaishvânara. In other words it may be stated that the nineteen organs (enumerated above) of the Universal Spirit in the manifest Universe, are on a macrocosmic scale (Adhidaivika), and each of them is respectively the source, the support and the resort of each of the similar organs of the different souls (Jivâtmâs) that are manifesting themselves in the different bodies on the microcosmic scale. In the wakeful state we enjoy things through the senses, and these consist of the gross nature, *i.e.*, the objective world. The wakeful state is called the first of the conditions of Âtmâ in the order of enumeration. In the evolution of the Universe, the wakeful state, *i.e.*, the gross manifestation, is the last state, and in the order of involution it is the first state, because the Dreamy state and state of Sound sleep, *i.e.* the subtle manifestation and the unmanifested states follow it. In analysing the Universe with the object of realizing the Âtmâ, it is the objective, that we have first to deal with, and hence it is called The First Condition.

स्वप्नस्थानोऽन्तःप्रज्ञः सप्ताङ्ग एकोनविंशतिमुखः प्रविविक्तभुक् तैजसो द्वितीयः पादः ॥ ४ ॥

S'RUTI (4).

The second condition is Taijasa, whose place is in the dreamy state, who is cognizant of the internal objects (ideas), who has seven members and nineteen mouths, and who enjoys the subtle (objects).

NOTE.

The mind is the source, the sustenance and the end of the five senses. When a man is awake, the soul is manifest in the senses; when he is asleep, the senses return to their fountain head the mind, and Âtmâ is seen manifest in the mind alone.

In dreamy sleep, when the senses are at rest, the mind is at work. The place of the mind in this state is in the luminary arteries which are 720,000,000 in number. These diffuse heat into the blood arteries and nervous system and are, therefore, called luminary. In the dreamy state it is said that the Âtmâ is seen manifest as diffused in internal nature, that is in the mind, and as the place of the latter is in the luminary arteries, the Âtmâ is called Taijasan (Luminous). The dreamer in a dreamy state creates a world of his own as well as a body for himself. The different objects of the dreamy world consist of ideas only, which, as compared with the matter of the wakeful world, are very fine and subtle, as they are the result of desire only. In this state, the Âtmâ has the same number of members of its body and the same number of mouths as in the wakeful state. But while a man lies asleep his Âtmâ is seen to have retreated from the outward perceptible world of five senses to the inner world of the mind, just as a man withdraws himself from the public view and retires to his inner or private apartments. It is, therefore, said that Âtmâ in the dreamy state is manifest in internal nature and enjoys objects made up of ideas which are comparatively fine.

यत्र सुप्तो न कञ्चन कामं कामयते न कञ्चन स्वप्नं पश्यति तत्सुषुप्तम् । सुषुप्तस्थान एकीभूतः प्रज्ञानघन एवानन्दमयो ह्यानन्दभुक् चेतोमुखः प्राज्ञस्तृतीयः पादः ॥ ५ ॥

S'RUTI (5).

When the sleeper courts no desire and sees no dream, it is sound sleep. He who in this state has become one, who has identified himself with one compact mass of knowledge, and who is full of bliss, who verily enjoys bliss, and whose mouth is consciousness is called Pra'jna. This is the third condition.

NOTE.

Every sensible person has the experience of sound sleep, and the reader has but to remember the experience of this state to understand this S'ruti. When we repose in the folds of sound sleep, all our knowledge of the wakeful and dreamy states is centred into oneness, or, in other words, all the knowledge of the wakeful and dreamy world becomes uniform, because in this state there is no conception of different objects : this has been called by some "chaos," by some "darkness," by some "the state of non-existence," and by others "Mûla-Prakriti" (the First Cause), or "Avyakta" (the unmanifested). But the reader should bear in mind that in this state, neither our entity, nor the objects of the wakeful and dreamy states are destroyed. It is one's own self that remains conscious of the existing state, and when we return from sound sleep to wakefulness, we remember and say that we slept a sound sleep. From this we know that the speaker in the first person, *i. e.* the Ego was not unconscious, but was rather conscious of the three states as unified. It is simply on account of the presence of Unity and absence of Multifariousness that the idea of seeming 'Chaos' or 'darkness' is conceived, giving rise to different theories relating to Âtmâ and the phenomenal world in this state. This S'ruti clears up the point and says that Âtmâ in this state, is conscious of the whole knowledge which has been moulded into oneness and reduced to a compact mass. As the different ornaments made up of a metal appear in so many different forms, but lose their identity and multifariousness when melted into a single compact mass, so, likewise, when Âtmâ withdraws from the wakeful sphere into the dreamy sphere, it takes along with itself the gross objective world, transformed into fine and subtle matter : and when it retires into the still inner apartment of the sphere of sound sleep, it takes with it the dreamy world in the form of a Molten Mass where on account of the compact nature of the dreamy world, no distinction can be made of the various objects which were displayed, when manifested in the external and mental spheres of consciousness. But, although the different forms of knowledge in their condensed state defy discernment, just as effects are not seen in their cause, we, nevertheless, know that all of them exist in a consolidated form, and it is the condensity of the wakeful and dreamy worlds that bars discrimination. Thus, what has been called by others darkness or the unconscious state, is found to be the store of knowledge, and when we awake we bring with us, out of this inexhaustible store, all the manifested nature. Being cognizant of this state of knowledge, the Âtmâ is called Prâjna or the knower of all. The sound sleep, as a matter of fact, is said to be full of bliss, though not absolute bliss. The Âtmâ being almost surrounded by bliss, enjoys of course bliss only. We have seen that in the first two conditions the Âtmâ enjoyed the gross and subtle matter with nineteen mouths, or organs of enjoyment already defined. In this state the only organ of enjoyment (mouth) is consciousness. Here we find a trinity, *viz.*, 'Âtmâ' the enjoyer, Ânanda (blissfulness) the thing enjoyed, and Chitta (consciousness) the organ of enjoyment. To sum up, we find here that the Ego (*i.e.* 'I') is conscious of Ânanda (blissfulness) only. The next S'ruti explains still further the state of Âtmâ in this condition.

एष सर्व्वेश्वर एष सर्व्वज्ञ एषोऽन्तर्य्याम्येष योनिः सर्व्वस्य प्रभवाप्ययौ हि भूतानाम् ॥ ६ ॥

S'RUTI (6).

He (the Pra'jna) is the Lord of all; He is omniscient; He is the internal ruler; He is the source of all; surely He is the origin and final resort of (all) beings.

NOTE.

As all the mental and physical worlds proceed from Âtmâ in his third condition, and all powers spring from him and are within his control, he is called the Lord of all; he is said to be omniscient, as here he is cognizant of the compact mass of knowledge, from which proceeds the Universe of variety. As Âtmâ knows the cause, he is said to know all the effects. In order to expand the compact mass into the visible and mental worlds, the Âtmâ does not exert from outside, nor does it require any instrument or materials to work with as a potter requires them to make a pot. It is said here that the Âtmâ is the internal ruler, who residing withim, controls every thing. He expands the contracted mass by virtue of his own law, just like a lotus that opens and shuts itself, or like a serpent that coils up or lengthens its own body. This state, when it expands, gives rise to the evolution of the manifested nature, and which, when it seemingly disappears, really draws back and finds a resort in its original source, in the same way as effects do in their cause. This condition is therefore the source and resort of all beings.

नान्तःप्रज्ञं न बहिःप्रज्ञं नोभयतःप्रज्ञं न प्रज्ञानघनं न प्रज्ञं नाप्रज्ञम् । अदृष्टमव्यवहार्य्यमग्राह्यमलक्षणमचिन्त्यमव्यपदेश्यमेकात्म्यमत्यसारं प्रपञ्चोपशमं शान्तं शिवमद्वैतं चतुर्थं मन्यन्ते स आत्मा स विज्ञेयः ॥ ७ ॥

S'RUTI (7)

The wise think *that* The Fourth, which is neither cognizant of internal nor external objects, nor of both ; which is not a compact mass of knowledge ; is neither intelligent nor unintelligent, is invisible, not acting, incomprehensible, undefinable, incogitable, indescribable, the sole essnece of I-am-ness (the one proof of the three states), with no trace of the conditioned world, all calm, all bliss, without duality. This is the Âtmâ, it should be known.

NOTE.

In this S'ruti the Âtmâ is shown in Its real existence, devoid of the three conditions, respectively called Vaishvânara, Taijasa, and Prâjna. It is, therefore, said that in this state, the Âtmâ is not seen diffused in external nature as we saw it in its first state called Vaishvânara (the wakeful state), nor manifest in internal nature, as it was in the dreamy state, termed as Taijasa. In one part of the dreamy state the Âtmâ is also said to be in the Transitional mood, which is a state between Vaishvânara and Prâjna. The Âtmâ here acts as I'shvara, the all powerful creative principle that creates everything it desires in the twinkle of an eye ; but, after having completed the creation, finds itself just in the same position as Vaishvânara in the waking state, subject to all laws Hence this state is called Transitional, standing between the First and the Third. Âtmâ as an entity is not one like Prâjna that may be described as being cognizant of the one compact mass of knowledge. When present in the third state, it is called Prâjna, but when freed from it, it is no longer called

Prâjna or Prajnânghana. Âtmâ when viewed as an entity, existing independently of the three states or conditions cannot be said to have intelligence ; but at the same time, being the reality of intelligence, as we find it when it is present in the three states, it cannot be said to be devoid of intelligence. It is said to be Invisible, being imperceivable by the senses. The position defined as 'Not acting' means, that the actor is not acting at the time. For instance, a carpenter when he is at work with his tools, is an actor, but when he lays aside his tools he is not acting. The Âtmâ is said to be 'Incomprehensible' as it is beyond the reach of the senses ; 'Undefinable,' as it has no qualities visible or invisible associated with its entity ; 'Incogitable' as it is beyond the scope of the contemplative organs· Manas (mind). As Âtmâ in its essential state has neither sound, touch, colour, taste or smell perceivable by the senses, has no visible or invisible qualities, nor is it seen in its real nature as manifested in the wakeful, dreamy or dreamless sleepy states. The Divine author has, therefore, called it 'Undescribable'.

The reader may have felt doubts here as to the very existence of Âtmâ. The S'ruti then clears up the doubt by saying that it is the essence of I-am-ness. This I-am-ness was present in the wakeful state ; it existed when the dreamy state took the place of the wakeful state ; and was also present in the state of sound sleep when the first two states had disappeared. And when the sound sleep changes into the wakeful state ; it still remains the same. The Ego does not change with the three states ; it remains the same throughout. This I-am-ness is the representative of Âtmâ in all the states. The essence of this I-am-ness is Âtmâ. In this essence we find no trace of the world which we have seen in the first three conditions. It is an embodiment of calmness and·bliss. The S'ruti goes further and says, it is Advaitam, which means 'without duality' or more literally 'without a second'. The word Advaitam signifies one that has not a second either of its own or of a different nature and is not composed of parts, that is to say it is a homogeneous whole in itself. This is the Âtmâ (the all pervading) whose existence the S'ruti requires us to realize.

सोऽयमात्माऽध्यक्षरमोङ्कारोऽधिमात्रम् । पादा मात्रा मात्राश्च पादा अकार उकार मकार इति ॥ ८ ॥

S'RUTI (8).

This Âtmâ is represented by the Syllable Aum, which in its turn is represented by Mâtrâs (letters). The conditions of Âtmâ are the Mâtrâs of Aum, and (conversely) the Mâtrâs of Aum are the conditions of Âtmâ The Mâtrâs are अ (A), उ (U), and म (M).

NOTE.

This S'ruti very clearly demonstrates that the Syllable Aum is a representative or Symbol of Âtmâ. It says that the substance denoted by the word Aum is the Âtmâ that has been alluded to in the Seventh S'ruti.

Now, as already shown, the Monosyllabic word Aum is made up of four parts. Three of these are Mâtrâs represented by letters, *viz.*, अ (A), उ (U) and म (M). The Fourth, which is spoken of as Be-ness in Chapter VII, Part I, is not represented by a Mâtrâ (symbol).

Again, it is said that the respective conditions of Âtmâ are truly represented by the Mâtrâs of the syllable Aum in the order given in the S'ruti.

The following S'rutis show the correspondence of each of the letters with the conditons of Âtmâ in their respective order.

जागरितस्थानो वैश्वानरोऽकारः प्रथमा मात्राऽऽप्तेरादिमत्त्वाद्वाऽऽप्नोति ह वै सर्वान् कामानादिश्च भवति य एवं वेद ॥ ९ ॥

S'RUTI (9).

Vaishvânara whose place is, in the waking state is (represented by) अ (A), the first Mâtrâ, from its

being all-pervading as well as being the first (letter). He who knows this verily obtains all desires ; (and) becomes the foremost.

NOTE.

Two reasons are given here to show that अ (A), Mâtrâ of Aum, is a fit representative of the wakeful condition, called Vaishvânara. The first of these is the pervasion of the elementary sound of अ (A) in all the letters of the Sanskrit Alphabet like the presence of the Vaishvânara (Universal Spirit) in all the things of the Universe. The second is, that it is the first letter in the formation of the syllable Aum, as the Vaishvânara is the first phase of Brahma.

We will first take into consideration the first similarity *viz.*, the pervasion of the letter अ (A) in all the letters of the Sanskrit Alphabet. We have already shown that all the vowels excepting उ (U) and the nasal sound of *Anuswâra* denoted by 'ng' or 'm' are made up of certain modifications of अ (A) or by the combination of अ (A) with उ (U) or by the combinations of modified sounds of अ (A) and उ (U) with some cansonantal sound. We will now show the presence of अ (A) in (U) and '.' or म्, the nasal sound denoted by '*ng*' or '*m*.'

Dr. Webster in his Dictionary gives the following definition of the letter A.————" A. The first letter of the Alphabet in most of the known languages of the earth. It is naturally the first letter, becuse it represents the first vocal sound naturally formed by the organs of speech, *viz.*, that heard in *far*, *mart* &c., being the sound uttered with a mere opening of the mouth without constraint and without any effort to alter the natural position or configuration of the lips."

As regards the sound of U or shorter sound of 'O,' Dr. Webster in his Principles of Pronunciation writes as follows :—

" § 24. Sound of O like OO short, marked O, as in *bosom*, *wolf*, *woman* &c. See § 8, Note, and § 27."

"§ 27. Regular short sound of OO, morked O͝O, O͝O, as in *wo͝ol*, *fo͝ot*; heard also in *wọlf*, *shọuld*, *bull* &c.—See § 8 Note."

"§ 8 Note. This is the extreme short sound of broad A, and coincides with the sound of O in *not* . . ."

We find that the sound of (अ) A "is the first vocal sound naturally formed by the organs of speech, and uttered with a mere opening of the mouth without constraint and without any effort to alter the natural position or configuration of the lips or the tongue." In the utterance of the sounds of all other letters excepting the nasal sound of '*ng*' or '*m*,' an effort is always made to alter the natural position or configuration of the vocal organs.

The Sanskrit Orthœpists have therefore given the name of अ (A) to the natural position of the organs of speech, as found in the utterance of the natural sound of अ (A) ; as all other sounds are a result of the alteration or modification of the natural position of the vocal organs, therefore the sounds of all other letters are only modifications of the sound of अ (A). We, however, find that in pronouncing short U as in 'put,' the voice takes its rise from the same place as in the case of अ (A); but when pronouncing उ (U) the voice rises upwards slightly, the lower lip is raised and the aperture between the lips is shortened. Thus the sound of उ (U) is simply a modification of the sound of अ (A). We have in this way shown that the sound of अ (A) pervades in all the vowels. Whether it pervades in the nasal sound represented by '*ng*' or '*m*' is to be next shown. We find that in uttering the nasal sound of Anuswâra '*ng*' or Makâra (M), the lips are closed and the sound continues until it comes to a stop. The only sound which can therefore be pronounced after the closing of the lips, is the nasal sound. The mouth including all its component parts is the organ of speech ; from it proceed all sounds, therefore, it is the receptacle of sounds. Its opening is denoted by the sound of the natural vowel अ (A), and its closing is denoted by the nasal sound (*ng*) or (*m*), the sound of अ (A) is therefore present in the closed mouth and is produced by its opening.

The nasal sound which is represented by a point (' · ') and is denoted by the closing of the organ of speech represents *Avyakta*, *i. e.*, the unmanifested state; its form of a dot is the source of all the forms, and the shutting of the mouth caused by its pronunciation is the source of all the sounds. We have now shown that अ (A) pervades in all the vowels. We will next show how the vowel अ (A) is present in all the consonants.

In the first part of this treatise, while analysing the syllable 'Aum' (ओम्), we confined our enquiry to vowels only, for the reason that, as the consonants depended for their very pronunciation on vowels, and had no separate existence of their own, it was considered needless to deal with them there. But, as in this S'ruti the letter अ (A) is stated to be pervading in all letters (Vowels and Consonants), it is well to now treat of them here.

We have seen that the natural vowel sound is अ (A), and having a sound of its own is undetermined *i. e.*, unrestricted; but when we determine the sound by any of the organs, a separate sound is produced, which is called a consonantal sound. For instance, when the vowel sound of अ (A) is stopped by the lips it is pronounced as 'Ap' 'Aph' 'ab' 'abh' 'Am' or as in Sanskrit 'pa,' 'pha ' 'ba, 'bha,' 'ma.' As these sounds are separate, separate forms are given to them, and are called consonantal sounds. But the linguists know that these sounds are no sounds at all, and were only determining or qualifying sounds of vowels, they therefore name these sounds as consonantal sounds, or such sounds as can be uttered only in conjunction with a vowel.

Thus the stoppage of the vowel sound by any of the Organs of Speech becomes the cause of a consonantal sound, and all the sounds created by the action of a certain organ, are named after that organ. Therefore the unrestricted vowel sounds determined by the lips are called labials ; by the palate, palatals ; by the teeth, dentals ; &c.

But we have already stated that the letters of the Alphabet are only symbols of sounds, and the names originally given to these letters were the actual sounds of the articulations that reached the ear. This original mode of pronunciation is preserved in the Sanskrit language, while in other languages the pronunciation of some of the letters is very much corrupted For instance, it is impossible for a stranger to know that the letter which is named in English 'Aich,' and denoted by the symbol 'h' has the pronunciation as pronounced in 'hand.' The consonant ब (B) is naturally pronounced as 'Ba' and not as 'Be' in English. If 'B,' as it is pronounced in English, be the representative of the sound of the *letter* 'B,' why should the *word* 'Be' be spelled with E affixed to B. From this we know that although B is pronounced as 'be,' still the actual value of the letter is its consonantal sound uttered with the vowel 'A' *i.e.* 'ba.' But as a consonant cannot be pronounced without the help of a vowel, therefore in the English language the vowel 'E' is affixed to B to pronounce it. We say the vowel 'E' is not the correct vowel to affix. As the pronunciation of the vowel 'A' is the first vocal sound naturally produced by the organs of speech, and all other sounds are produced only by a change of the natural position of the vocal organs, it is, therefore, very reasonable to say that the only vowel that can naturally be used with all the consonants without modifying the consonantal sound is the vowel 'A.'

It may be said that Sanskrit has a very complete and perfect Alphabet. We have already shown that it has a greater number of vowels than any other language, and it will now be shown that it has also the greatest number of consonants in its vocabulary. It is, for this reason only, that words of different foreign languages can be transliterated into Sanskrit characters expressing, comparatively speaking, the exact pronunciation of the words as pronounced in the original languages.

The Sanskrit consonants are pronounced with the help of the first vowel अ (A), which is also contained in the formation of the characters, without the necessity of making any addition to or alteration in them, while in affixing other vowels to them a modification in the form of the characters is required. If, however, we want to show that a consonant at the end of a word is to be pronounced without the vowel अ (A), we subtract the vowel from the last letter by cutting it with a dash, for example, in order to show that म is without the vowel अ we will write it as म्. And if any other vowel sound is to be affixed, the sign of that particular vowel will be added to it, modifying the form of the consonant. We give below a list of the consonants, and their pronunciation in Roman characters :—

क	ख	ग	घ	ङ	च	छ	ज	झ	ञ
ka	kha	ga	gha	ṇga*	cha	chha	ja	jha	ṇja*
ट	ठ	ड	ढ	ण	त	थ	द	ध	न
ṭa	ṭha	ḍa	ḍha	ṇa	ta	tha	da	dha	na
प	फ	ब	भ	म	य	र	ल	व	श
pa	pha	ba	bha	ma	ya	ra	la	va	sha
		ष			स	ह	ज्ञ		
		ṣḥa or-kḥa			sa	ha	jna.		

Now the reader will find that all the consonants given above are pronounced with the elementary vowel sound अ (A). Hence the vowel अ (A) from its root 'apalri,' means pervading, as it prevades in all letters.

Just as we have seen the pervasion of अ (A) in all the letters, we have, likewise, seen the pervasion of the Universal Spirit (Vaishvânara) in the Universe. We, thus, find an exact similarity of the all-pervading quality of the first Mâtrâ अ (A) of the monosyllable ओम् (Aum) with that of the Vaishvânara, the first condition of the Âtmâ.

The second similarity is, that अ (A) being the first natural sound, is the first letter of the Alphabet and the first Mâtrâ (letter) of the syllable Aum (ओम्). Similarly Vishva or

* Nasal Sound.

Vaishvânara is the first of the phases in which Âtmâ is known as manifested in the Universe. Both the Vaishvânara and the Mâtrâ अ being the first of their kind in their respective spheres, the second similarity exists between the letter अ (A) and the Vaishvânara condition of Âtmâ.

Having found a symbol of Vaishvânara in the letter अ (A) the S'ruti in a way speaks of the mode of contemplating on the Vaishvânara, and enumerates the benefits that arise from this process of contemplation. It should be borne in mind that there is a difference in the knowledge of Âtmâ (Janâna) and mere meditation on it (Dhyâna). The knowledge of Âtmâ is that state of consciousness in which the real existence of Âtmâ is fully realized by one's ownself without the help of a symbol.

The terms 'Upâsnâ' and 'meditation' have been defined in the first part, where it is shown that no meditation can be made unless the subject of meditation be present before the meditator, or a symbol of it, whether perceptible by the senses or conceivable by the mind. The meditation is not said to be complete until the meditator fully realizes the thing meditated upon. Take, for instance, the well known example of Majnu, who had an extreme love for Leila. One day, while meditating upon Leila, he so identified himself with her that he lost conciousness of himself. While he was in this state, some one called to him aloud several times by his name. But Majnu heard him not; his mind being wholly concentrated on Leila, he had lost altogether the idea of his own existence. Thereupon the person was told by an acquaintance of Majnu to call him by the name of Leila, his beloved one: this done, Majnu at once responded to the call. This example shows that the meditator had identified himself exactly with the subject of his meditation.

The Upanishad says at the outset that Aumkâra is Brahma, and this Aumkâra is the subject of our meditation. This meditation is considered as the highest and the best, as it leads to the removal of Vikshepa (unsteadiness of mind) and ultimately to the knowledge of Âtmâ.

As Âtmâ which forms the subject of our meditation, is not a perceptible or a conceivable object, we require a comprehensive representative, which may serve as a symbol, having corresponding semblances and analogies. The Vedas and Upanishads tell us that such a representative is to be found in the monosyllabic word Aum (ओम्). By following and contemplating this symbol with its analogies and semblances, we will attain the knowledge of Âtmâ itself.

As the word Aum (ओम्) is said to be the representative of Âtmâ, so the Mâtrâs composing this word are also representatives respectively of the different conditions in which Âtmâ manifests itself. The S'ruti says that अ Mâtrâ of ओम् is representative of the Vaishvânara, the first condition. Having the symbol अ (A) before him, the meditator is to continue contemplating on the Vaishvânara, till he identifies himself with the subject of his meditation.

It has been seen that अ (A) pervades in all the letters of the Alphabet, and Vaishvânara in all things of the Universe. Let us now see how the meditator can attain his end of identification. Knowing that the Universe is composed of individual things, we are to find out what is common to all things in the Universe. Our inquiry shows that every individual thing has a body and, therefore, we conclude that the condition of Embodiment is common to all the different individuals.

The contemplator has also a body, and his egoism is at present confined to his own body alone. Thus, he finds that Embodiment is Omnipresent throughout the material Universe, just as अ (A) pervades all the letters of the alphabet. In his meditation on Vaishvânara, he should contemplate on the Omnipresence of Âtmâ in the Universe, manifested and diffused in the form of Embodiment in all the substances of the Universe. The subject of his meditation, therefore is Embodiment, which is also present in him. So by continued contemplation and meditation, he identifies himself with the All-Embodiment, and then begins to think that he is actually the abstract quality of Embodiment. Prior to this, his egoism was confined only to his body, but now by dint of meditation, his I-am-ness is extended to All-Embodiment, which has been shown to be common to all things, and therefore Omnipresent in the Universe, as no matter can exist without some form: the Embodiment, therefore, is the principal thing by which the individuality of things can be conceived or perceived by the senses, but the Embodiment being in itself an abstract quality, having no multifarious forms, is found to be uniform throughout the Universe. From the subtile, invisible atom to the enormously huge mountains, all things are within the reach of this All-Pervading Embodiment. In other words, we say that all things exist in Embodiment and the meditator, having by the strength of meditation identified himself with Embodiment, finds that all the qualifications of Embodiment are assimilated in him, and it is for this reason, that in this state of meditation, he realizes that he is prevading in all things; that all things are reachable to him and that all things exist in him; thus, his egoism is now extended to the Universe. This is what we call the meditation on the first Mâtrâ of ओम् (Aum), representing the Vaishvânara phase of Âtmâ.

Let us contemplate on the Omnipresence of Vaishvânara in another way. My egoism is at present confined to my body only, which is composed of five elements. I also find that all things in the Universe are composed of the same five elements. It follows from this that the same five elements are Omnipresent in the Universe. In this way, I find that the five elements are commonly found in the universe as well as in my body. I will now meditate on the Omnipresence of the five elements, till I am able to identify myself with the said elements. My egoism which was first confined to the elements composing my body alone, has now been extended to the elements composing the universe. And as all things are made up of the same elements, and as all things are within their scope, so I see, by the light of my meditation, that all things are made up of the elements composing myself, and are therefore within my reach. The popular fallacy consists in limiting Egoism to individual bodies in which they see their soul manifest at the time. We say that Âtmâ is All-Pervading, and exists everywhere. The Âtmâ is not limited to any single body alone, but it is All in all. The folly of limiting egoism to particular objects is a misunderstanding (Ajnâna), and this is what gives rise to our miseries aad troubles. Look for instance, at the case of a man who is sitting on the parapet of a house. On being asked as to where is he sitting, he replies 'on the wall.' He thus limits his egoism to the wall. But we ask, Does not this wall stand on the surface of the earth ? Is the wall apart and separated from the earth ? We know it for certain, that the wall is not separated from the earth ; but if the man on the wall were to say that he is sitting on tha sphere of this earth, people would laugh at him. In this case we see that the man is laughed at for speaking the truth, because it does not correspond with the popular idea.

We now see that the Âtmâ (Self) of the body is not confined to this body, as the man on the wall is not cofined to the wall. By making this assertion, I do not limit the egoism of the man on the wall to the wall, or to the house, or to the town, or to the country, or to any particular continent of the world, but rather say that his egoism extends to the whole earth, nay to the whole universe, the great Cosmos itself. Now the question is whether the earth goes to make up the grand building of the universe or not ? The answer is that it does. If so, is not an inhabitant of the earth an inhabitant of the universe ? No one can dare deny this truth. As a man, while actually occupying a space of, say a couple of yards or less, in one of the various rooms of a grand bulding, is said to be occupying the whole of the house ; similarly, there is no harm in saying that I am the occupant of the universe. If you are not astonished to hear that an Emperor occupies a big Imperial Palace (while he actually never occupies a greater space than the length and breadth of his body), there should be no surprise felt when it is said that I occupy the universe. In the first case the egoism was extended from a yard or two to thousands of yards, and in the second case it is extended to a countless number of yards. If the latter is impossible, then the first must also be impossible. But the first is believed to be true, then why should not the second also be believed to be so. In the present day we find that instead of placing the senses under the subordination of intelligence, we, on the contrary, subject our intelligence to the supremacy of our senses. By this I mean to say that we believe the ideas conveyed to us by our senses, without allowing the intellect to act as a judge and to perform its functions of discrimination. The conclusions drawn by our intelligence are always sound, while the conclusions drawn by our senses are often misleading. The sense of vision betrays to us a serpent in a rope, and the beauty of a watery surface in a waterless desert as in the case of a mirage.

We will dwell here a little longer on the difficult subject of meditation. It may be stated that the idea of pervasion is of two kinds, viz., the sensory and the intellectual. In the first case, we perceive the pervasion actually by our senses, in the second the senses show the pervasion of a thing in a part only, while the intellect shows it in the whole. We will try to illustrate this by an example :—A large building catches fire in one corner of a room, the watchman of the house runs to the owner who is at a short distance and informs him of the alarming news that the house is on fire. The watchman means to say, and the owner understands, that the whole building is on fire, although the watchman has actually seen and the by-standers actually see that only a part of the building is on fire; nevertheless, everybody says that the building is on fire. Here the sensory idea of pervasion is subjected to the discretionary power of intellect. Again, we see a crow sitting on a part of one of the branches of a large tree. This is the perception conveyed to us by our vision, but by the intellectual idea of pervasion we say that the crow is sitting on the tree.

Take another example :—Our sight shows to us the dial of the sun not much bigger than a common plate, and not having a larger diameter than a span or so, but the science of

14

astronomy teaches us that the sun has a diameter of 888,646 miles as compared with 7,926 miles, the diameter of our earth. This shows that the sun is about 112 times bigger than the earth. Now, intellectually, we have a certain belief that the sun is bigger than the earth, but still our vision causes us to think that the sun is not much bigger than a common plate. Likewise, although my own Âtmâ is everything in all things, and pervades the whole of the unlimited universe, yet on account of the defectiveness of the sensitive organs, I am seen confined to a single body. By meditation I have come to know that I am all-pervading, but the senses still show me as limited only to this mortal body. This is called illusion (विपर्यास), which is seeing something different from what it really is.

The Vishva, *i.e.* a man in his wakeful state, is subjected first to illusion, that is to say seeing things in a different light from what they actually are, and secondly to ignorance, which means non-realization of the real and actual state of existence. By the power of meditation and keen intellect, we remove illusion and ignorance, and realize that Vishva and Vaishvânara are the different names of the one and the same entity.

What has been stated above may be described in another way. We have said that अ (A) pervades in all the letters, and Embodiment in all the bodies of the Universe. If the reader pictures to himself the whole Universe as a single body, he will understand that every single thing forms a componant part of the Universe. If my single body, to which my egoism is limited, be excluded from this Universe, the present Universe cannot be said to exist in its present complete form. To explain symbollically, let us suppose this Universe to be denoted by 'a' and my individual body by 'b.' Let us allow, for the sake of argument, that:my body is excluded from the Universe ; the Universe then will no more be expressed as 'a' but rather as 'a-b.' It is no more the same Universe, if there exists outside of it even the smallest thing possible. Therefore, the reader will see that the exclusion of my single body breaks down the huge and vast structure of the Virâta (universal body). If then, the whole of the existing Virâta is dependent for its present existence on my body, it follows that my body has a value which is equivalent to that of a centre in a circle. The manifested Universe is, for argument's sake, compared to a circle, though there is a difference between the Vîrâta circle and a circle drawn on a board; inasmuch as the former has a centre everywhere, but its circumference nowhere, while the latter has a known circumference and a known centre. And so I am the centre of the Virâta circle which has no definable circumference. All the bodies around me in the Universe are, therefore, emanations from me, as all lines in the circle, drawn from the centre to the circumference, are emanations from the central point. When I am the centre of the Virâta, and all the Universe depends for its existence on me, it may be correctly stated that the various things in the Virâta are only of me, and all of them are within my reach, all of them being emanations from me. As the circumference and all the lines and figures in a circle bear testimony to the greatness of their source, the centre, so, all the Universe bears testimony to my grandeur, I being the centre of Virâta. If the centre be lost, the circle is lost, but if the centre stands and the circle is lost, no harm whatever is done, we can draw another circle. In the same way, if the circle of Virâta be destroyed, I can create another Virâta circle. In other words, it means that "the centre of Parbrahma is everywhere and its circumference nowhere."

When I find that I am the cause of the present Virâta, and that it exists in me and finally disappears in me, it may truly be said that the Virâta is only a *glory* of mine, as it has no existence independent of myself. Thus, the reader will see that all things in the Virâta are within me. By this argument is realized the truth of the assertions made in the S'ruti, that whosoever meditates on the pervasion of Âtmâ, represented by अ (A) mâtrâ of ओम् (Aum) undoubtedly obtains the gratification of all his desires.

The next similarity stated by the S'ruti between अ (A) mâtrâ of ओम् (Aum) and the Vaishvânara condition of Âtmâ, is that of their respectively being the first in their own states. We see that अ (A) is the first letter of the alphabet and the fi rst mâtrâ of ओम् (Aum). Likewise, Vaishvânara is the first phase, of Âtmâ in our enquiry of Brahma. The S'ruti says that whosoever meditates on the priority of the Vaishvânara phase, represented by अ (A), mâtrâ of ओम् (Aum), becomes foremost of all.

The reader will have undoubtedly realized the truth of this assertion, when he finds that the meditator considers himself to be the centre, the first cause of Virâta. When I say I am the centre, the cause of the Virâta, I very clearly mean to say that I am the beginning of everything, and that all things are posterior to me. These truths are realized through meditation ; and the benefit derived from it is that the meditator becomes contented and calm in mind, that he then realizes the true conception of the expressions :—

"Thou art in me, and I in thee," "I in them and thou in me," "I am Alpha and Omega, the beginning and the end, the first and the last."

The Eastern Monism, or the Advaitism of the Upanishads, which treats of the unity in multiplicity and multiplicity in unity, is the only true philosophy that combines both science and philosophy. The knowledge of this alone, which is called Brahma-Vidyâ, can guide a man to the path of true liberation from all misery and future births.

स्वप्नस्थानस्तैजस उकारो द्वितीया मात्रोत्कर्षादुभयत्वाद्वोत्कर्षति ह वै ज्ञानसन्ततिं समानश्च भवति नास्याब्रह्मवित्कुले भवति य एवं वेद ॥ १० ॥

S'RUTI (10).

Taijasa, whose sphere is the dreamy state, is represented by उ (U), the second Mâtrâ, on account of its being of a more elevated nature, as well for as the reason that it occupies an intermediate position

He who knows this, verily advances the progress of knowledge, and (being thus enlightened) is in harmony with all, and none of his descendants will be ignorant of Brahma

NOTE.

In this S'ruti it is stated that Âtmâ in its Taijasa condition is represented by the letter उ (U), the second mâtrâ of ओम् (Aum). The letter उ (U) with (त) affixed to it means उत्कर्ष (Utkarsh), signifying elevation or exaltation. Thus, there is a similarity between the symbol उ (meaning elavation) and the Âtmâ herein called Taijasa. The dreamy state is an elevated one, as compared with the wakeful ; because, in the latter, Atmâ was manifest in gross external matter, and its enjoyment in that state was also of a gross material nature. In the dreamy state, Âtmâ resides in fine luminous matter, and the things which it enjoys here are finer in nature viz., ideas and knowledge.

The second similarity is that the letter उ (U) in the syllable ओम् (Aum), stands between अ (A) and म (M), as Taijasa stands intermediate between Vishva and Prâjna.

The above two similarities find an easy explanation in the form and sound of the letters अ (A), उ (U) and ' ं ' (*ng* or M).

The science of mathematics teaches us that a point is that which has neither length, nor breadth, nor magnitude, and that a line is length without breadth. It also tells us that if several points be placed lengthwise, a line will be formed. But we find that all the various possible mathematical figures and diagrams are produced by the modification of a line. The source of all the figures and diagrams is, therefore, a point. These points and lines, as defined above, are simply ideal, but we nevertheless denote them by certain marks. A point, for instance, is denoted by a dot ' . ' and the model of a line is always drawn in the form of a perpendicular or a horizontal line, as/or —.

The theory inculcated in S'rutis 9, 10 and 11 is, that the nasal sound of Anuswâra is denoted by a point; that this point contains all the possible figures in the world, that when it expands, it takes the form of a straight line, which in the Sanskrit language is the symbol of the vowel अ (A). As the sounds of all the letters are the modifications of the sound of अ (A), likewise, the form of all the letters is a modification of the straight line, the symbol of the letter अ (A). In fixing forms for all the different letters, the above fact was particularly kept in view, and it is for this reason, as will appear by a glance at the Sanskrit letters, that all the different modifications of the straight line, representing different letters do not stand by themselves, but are annexed to a straight line (the symbol of अ) placed at the head of each figure, excepting the Ayogvah letters, *viz.,* Anuswâra (nasal sound) and Visargini (guttral sound). The real symbol of उ (U) in Sanskrit is written as the figure within brackets (ᵕ). This form clearly shows that the lower part of the perpendicular line has been raised higher into a semi-circular form, just as the sound has been raised in its pronunciation. In pronouncing the sound of the letter अ (A) the mouth is simply opened, and the sound flows therefrom in a *straight line,* which is the symbol of its sound. In pronouncing the letter उ as 'U' in 'put' the sound, instead of flowing out straight, is raised higher and the lower lip is raised upwards, and the aperture caused by the opening of the mouth is shortened. Just as the mouth is shaped in a particular form in pronouncing उ (U), similarly the straight line is formed into a circular shape, the lower end rising upwards. In other words, it means that the point which has been expanded into a line, is again to be concentrated and to take its original form of a point. But in the form of उ (U) we find that it stands midway between the form of a point and the form of a line. In reducing the line to a point, the form of उ (ᵕ) stands midway.

Having seen that उ (U) is a good representative of Taijasa, we will now proceed to state briefly the mode of meditation contemplated in this S'ruti.

In the wakeful state I identified myself with Vaishvânara, by contemplating that I was nothing but the 'Embodiment' which was common to all the bodies in the Universe. Now, we see that all the phenomenal world that appears to us in a dream is made up of knowledge (or ideas) only. It may be noted here that there are two conditions in which knowledge exists, *viz.*, one without motion and the other in motion as ideas. For example, as bubbles that rise in water are nothing but water modified by wind, so ideas are similarly nothing but knowledge moved by will-power. When knowledge is in motion, the mind is said to be at work; and in the wakeful state the action of the mind is either applied towards a particular perceptible object or to imaginary objects, as, for instance, when employed in building airy castles. In the dreamy state also, the knowledge is not at rest, and therefore the mind is at work. The phenomena of a dream appear to be as real and actual as the things of the wakeful world. In the wakeful world, which we comparatively call more real, we see that the food which we eat fills the stomach, and thus appeases hunger; the water we drink quenches thirst; we have the feeling of joy or pain; we take a horse, mount him, and make a journey; we kill a man with a sword, and so on. In the wakeful state, by the force of imagination, we sometimes draw living pictures of things, but as our imagination is not then working quite independently of our senses, the picture of our imagination does not serve our purpose so well as things of the wakeful world which we call real. But in dreamy state we find that the things of our imagination serve all the purposes, as do the things of the wakeful objective world. We find that in a dream the food we eat appeases our hunger, the water quenches our thirst, the horse takes the rider hundreds of miles away, and so on. Therefore, on waking we say that such and such appeared to us in a dream as clearly as seen in a wakeful state. We will now make enquiries as to the substance of which the things in a dream are formed. We sleep on a small limited bed, but in a dream we see all the universe with a sun, moon, stars and the seemingly objective world. The things we see in a dream do not appear unreal at the time. We fear a serpent and a lion as much as we do in the wakeful world. But we know that in the wakeful state we are conscious of the external physical world, and enjoy external gross things with our nineteen organs of enjoyment. In the dreamy state, though the senses and organs of the dreamer are considered to be at rest and without motion, the dreamer instantaneously creates, out of his own consciousness, a seemingly objective world with all its objects, as well as a body of his own to enjoy the same. This is the internal world made of very fine matter, inasmuch as the Universe of unlimited expanse exists in the fine imperceivable arteries. The enjoyment of the internal world in the dreamy state is, therefore, said to be subtle. The substance of which the dreamy world is made up is, knowledge. In sound sleep this knowledge is at rest, and this state is ordinarily known as a state of darkness or ignorance. But when this very knowledge, considered to be darkness or ignorance in sound sleep, is agitated into motion, it takes the form of a dream. In this state evolution had commenced, and we find that the elements are yet single-fold and without proper arrangement. The forms we see in a dream are composed of simple subtile elements, which in their turn become the parents of grosser elements. The ether is an omnipresent element, and the air (gases) which comes out of ether is omnipresent in the rest of the elements, and neither of them has a visible colour or form. The elements which have a colour or form are earth (solids), water (liquids), and fire (heat). The elements which we see in the wakeful world are harmoniously arranged together, and each of the simple elements that we see is really a compound of the three elements that have a form, together with air (gases) and ether. The earth contains earth, water, and fire. The water contains water, earth, and fire. The fire which we see contains fire, earth, and water. What we call simple elements are, therefore, triples in themselves, and these triples are again combined to make compounds. In the dreamy world, things, bodies, and their enjoyment are all subtle, while in the wakeful state they are gross. Everybody knows that the things of the dreamy world are made up of imagination or rather knowledge in motion. Our bodies, as well as the things enjoyed, are all made up of ideas, *i. e.* knowledge in motion. Therefore, in meditating upon Taijasan we see that the thing common here is knowledge only. I, therefore, identify myself with knowledge which is common to all. In meditating on the wakeful condition, I contemplated that I was Embodiment, but now when I meditate upon the condition of the dreamy state, I contemplate that I am no more a lifeless Embodiment, but that I am knowledge. The Embodiment was a lifeless abstract thing, and knowledge is life and consciousness; and it is by the force of my meditation, that I now realize myself as knowledge, of which all things of the dreamy world are made up. Thus, by this mode of contemplation, I am elevated. The object of my meditation in the first state was Embodiment, while in the present condition it is knowledge. From a lifeless component of the Universe, I find myself the life of the Universe. Now, when I realize in myself that I am knowledge, the cause of the Universe, I identify myself with that state in which Brahma is called Hiranyagarbha, the creator of the universe.

Now to treat of the 2nd similarity. उ (U), occupying an intermediate position, partakes of the sound of अ (A) and म् (M) in the pronunciation of Aum or Om(ओम्). Likewise Âtmâ as Taijasa appears to partake of the attributes of Prâjna and of Vishva, namely, almightiness and limited power respectively. Hence, we find that in the dreamy state the Taijasa first acts the part of an Almighty Creator, because, in the twinkling of an eye, he creates the universe together with all its requirements, and then, limiting himself to a single body, partakes of the nature of Vishva. In the latter garb, he fears the lion and a serpent of his own creation, which appear and disappear in the knowledge of the dreamer. This stage, attributed to Âtmâ, called Taijasan, is intermediate between Vishva and Prâjna, as उ (U) is intermediate between अ and म् (A and M).

The first fruit of this meditation is, that the meditator receives enlightenment, and increases knowledge. The reader, I think, will have no difficulty in realizing this when he has seen that the contemplator has identified himself at this stage with knowledge and Hiranyagarbha. The second fruit of this meditation is that he becomes harmonized with all, and bears no enmity towards the one nor love for the other. He now finds that the Universe is the creation of his own knowledge, and, therefore, not separate from him. He does not now fear a serpent, a lion, a ghost or an apparition, as he finds all of them composed of the same matter (knowledge) as he has in himself. Do you think that if a man in a dreamy state knew that the serpent and the lion of his dream were nothing but creatures of his own imagination, having no antagonistic existence of their own, he would be afraid of them ; or knowing that the king he sees in a dream is a form of his imagination, he would pay him any respect; or knowing that wealth and kinsmen are also the creation of his own imagination, he would love them or be sorry for their seeming loss? I say he will see harmony in all, and will neither dread the one, nor respect the other, nor love and grieve for the third. The third fruit is, that the offspring of the meditator of Ukâra Mâtrâ or Taijasa will never remain ignorant of the knowledge of Brahma. This is also a natural conclusion, because the son of a wise man is naturally expected to be wise. The father takes care generally to bring up his son in his own ways. There is nobody usually speaking so dear to a man in this world as a son to his father. Such being the case, the father will necessarily teach his son the same mode of meditation, and the son, by meditating in the manner the father has done, will also become a wise man and in time the knower of Brahma. This is the second mode of meditation which is higher than the first. The fruits of these modes of meditation are realized by meditators through meditation only. By the first mode, the meditator's egotism is extended to the whole of the Universe, and the result is *contentment*. By the second mode the meditator finds himself *identified* with knowledge or consciousness, and becomes a *wise man* and *harmonized* to all.

सुषुप्तस्थानः प्राज्ञो मकारस्तृतीया मात्रा । मितेरपीतेर्वामिनोति ह वा इद ॅं सर्व्वमपीतिश्च भवति य एवं वेद ॥ ११ ॥

S'RUTI (11).

Prâjna, whose sphere is sound sleep, is represented by (म्) (M) the third Mâtrâ, from its being the measure as well as from its being resort (of all). He who knows this, verily measures this all, and becomes the resort (of all).

NOTE.

Two similarities are stated in this S'ruti between the Prâjna state of Âtmâ and the *Makâra Mâtrâ* of Aum. The one is that of being the measure, and the other that of being the resort. We have already said that the pronunciation of the monosyllable Aum ends with the nasal '*ng*,' otherwise denoted by M, and have also shown that this is the only vowel that can be pronounced with the lips shut, and that the sound of A unites with the sound of U ; and the mixed sound of A and U, *viz.* O (ओ), merges into the sound of म् (M). The sound of O is not destroyed, but as it retires into the sound of M it becomes imperceivable. As *Makâra Mâtrâ* (M) has the capacity of holding within itself the other two Mâtrâs, *viz.*, '*Akâra*' (A) and *Ukâra* (U), therefore *Makâra* is truly said to be a measure by which the other two are measured, just as we see that the measure of 10 seers is contained in a measure of 20 seers, and the latter is contained in a measure of one maund, *i. e.* 40 seers. But one maund is the standard measure by which 10 seer and 20 seer weights are measured, the latter being only its fractions. So M being the denominator and A and U being the numerators, the latter are measured by the former. Therefore, when we say that the one disappears into the other, we do not mean that the existence of the first is annihilated, but rather we use the expression in the same sense, as when we say that the smaller measure is lost sight of in the greater measure. In this case M measures out both A and U, because it is pronounced by the organs of speech in their undisturbed position. This position of the organs possesses the capacity of pronouncing all the vocal sounds. Therefore, it is the highest vocal measure by which all the other sounds are measured. This position of the organs of speech may be compared to a closed box containing different things. As the box is the measure of all the things contained in it, so M is the measure of all the sounds; because all other different sounds are its modifications and are produced by causing a change in this, which is the natural position of the vocal organs. For this reason *Makâra Mâtrâ* is called the source and resort of all the sounds. The S'ruti says, that this attribute of M has a similarity with Prâjna, the third stage of Âtmâ, represented by dreamless sleep. As अ (A), when it unites with उ (U), apparently loses its own pronunciation, and exists in a subtle and imperceivable form in the compound ओ (O), so the wakeful world seems to disappear into the dreamy world; that is to say, ths grosser things exist there in a subtler form, and are lost sight of in the higher and lighter measure of subtility. As the compound of A and U (*viz.*, O) merges into the higher measure म (M), so do the dreamy and wakeful worlds seem to lose their existence in the dreamless sleepy state. The nasal sound is considered to be a consolidation of all the sounds, so is this third stage a consolidation of the first two. As A and U exist in M, so the wakeful and dreamy worlds exist in the third stage, but they exist, as effects exist in their cause, or as the forms of the different vessels exist in their cause, the earth, of which they are formed; and as the closed form of Anuswâra symbolized by a point (•) is the measure of all the letter forms, so the first cause Prajnâna-Ghana is the measure of both the first named worlds. As the closed form of a point, the symbol of Anuswâra, by its expansion takes the different forms of letters, and the letters take the form of words, so does the Prajnâna-Ghana (state of one compact mass of knowledge) by process of evolution take the modified forms of the dreamy and wakeful worlds.

The second similarity is that of being the resort. The Sanskrit word अपीति *Apiti* from its very root means 'retiring into Self.' The substratum to which certain things retire and in which they afterwards exist, is called the resort of those things. If all the lines drawn from a centre be retracted to the centre, it is called concentration. When there arise different modifications of mind, it becomes diffused in the external world, and takes the form of things perceived through its subordinate sensory organs. It is concentration when the mind is at rest, and does not undergo modifications. We have seen that *Makâra* (M) is the source and the terminus of all the vocal sounds wherein the latter exist as effects do in their cause. Therefore, Makâra (M) is the resort of all the sounds.

Similarly, the wakeful and dreamy worlds take their rise from the condition called Prajnâna-Ghana, and retreat to the same source ; and then exist there as effects exist in their cause (*viz.*, in the form of cause itself). It is for this reason that Prajnâna-Ghana is said to be the source as well as the resort of both the wakeful and the dreamy worlds. Let us now explain the mode of meditation as contemplated in the S'ruti. It has been already shown that the matter of which the world is made up consists of knowledge. There are three states of this knowledge, *viz.*, (1) unmanifest to the mind (2) manifest to mind only, and (3) manifest to mind through the senses. In the first state it is seemingly motionless, and in the next two states it is in motion. It has also been shown that the dreamy sleep or the mental world is an evolution from the dreamless sleep, and the wakeful world is in its turn evolved from the mental world; and that in their retreat, the wakeful world disappears into the mental (dreamy), and the mental into the unmanifest. The unmanifest is, therefore, a consolidation of the other two, or, in other words, one compact mass of knowledge. In our meditation of the Vaishvânara state, we identified ourselves with the Vaishvânara by contemplating that we were 'Embodiment,' which was common to all the different bodies of the Universe. In our meditation of Âtmâ in the second stage, called Taijasa or Hiranyagarbha (the enjoyer of the dreamy state), we found that all the substances of the dreamy Universe were composed of knowledge existing in us, and we identified ourselves with knowledge in motion. Now we have seen that in the third stage there is a consolidation of knowledge from which the dreamy and the wakeful worlds take their rise and into which these finally retire, as it is the source and resort of all. When the contemplator realizes himself as being the source and resort of all, he identifies himself with the I'shwara or Avyâkrit (the unmanifested state). The following are the benefits of this meditation :—

(i). That the meditator measures out all that exists.

(ii). That he retires into himself.

The reader remembers well that the benefit of meditation is to be enjoyed through meditation only. Therefore, when a man contemplates and identifies himself with Prajnâna-Ghana or Avyâkrit, he naturally considers himself as the source of all things, and, as such, measures out all things of the universe which he contemplates to be his own manifestation. As regards the second benefit, we say that things are said to retire when they return to their original state, *i. e.* to their source. Likewise, when the contemplator realizes himself as the resort of all the Universe, he naturally feels an apathy for things of the manifested world, and retreats to his Avyâkrit state. The apparent benefit, which the contemplator will derive in the wakeful world, will be that his mind will always be at rest, and that all the Vikshepa, *i.e.* restlessness, will cease. Because restlessness and uneasiness remain only so long as a man thinks that the things which he sees are existing apart and separately from his own Self. But knowing that all things have originally evolved from him in his third stage, he finds rest.

अमात्रश्चतुर्थोऽव्यवहार्य्यः प्रपंचोपशमः शिवोऽद्वैत एवमोङ्कार आत्मैव संविशत्यात्मनाऽऽत्मानं य एवं वेद य एवं वेद ॥ १२ ॥

S'RUTI (2).

The Fourth is Amâtra (Unmarked). It is not acting, has no trace of the conditioned world, is all Bliss and without duality. This verily is Aumkâra. He who knows this, verily he who knows this, enters into his own Self by means of the same Self.

NOTE.

In treating of the letters of ओम् (Aum), we have shown that, besides three letters अ (A), उ (U), and म् (M), there is a fourth component, which has no symbol in form and speech. This is denoted only by Be-ness, and this Be-ness is present in the whole word ओम् (Aum) as well as in its component parts. Equivalent to this Amâtra, *i.e.* Be-ness of Aum (ओम्), is *The Fourth i. e.* the Âtmâ itself. The first three were the states in which the Âtmâ appeared to us as respectively qualified by those states, *viz*., the Vaishvânara, the Taijas, and the Prâjna. The entity which was seen in these states is here called *The Fourth*, with no qualifications about it. *The Fourth* is the unqualified entity, *viz*., the Âtmâ.

The expressions *not-acting, having no trace of the conditioned world, all-bliss, without duality*, have already been commented upon in the 7th S'ruti. In this S'ruti it is said that this Aumkâra, *The Fourth*, is Âtmâ, with no qualifying state. In the last three S'rutis the Upâsanâ or meditation on Âtmâ, as required in its first three stages (called Vaishvânara, Taijasa and Prâjna), was laid down, but in the present S'ruti we find no Upâsanâ of *The Fourth*, because, in Upâsanâ we require either the original itself or a representative of the thing meditated upon; and there can be no representative or symbol unless there be some qualities in the subject of meditation ; but as *The Fourth* is the entity without any qualities whatever, it cannot form a subject of visual or mental meditation. This entity can only be realized in the way described in the Vedas; the general way in which this is done is, by taking each of the abstract qualities into consideration and finding that It is neither this nor that, and that It is none of these ; and that Its existence can only be denoted by the word Be-ness, by which we mean that It, exists, but as this existence has no qualities, we are unable to give any description of It except by allusion and saying that Âtmâ is an entity which exists always and everywhere, which is unchangeable, without a second, is not subject to time, and is independent of all. This S'ruti, assuming that the contemplator has, by the modes of meditation mentioned in the preceding three S'rutis, become a capable student of Brahma, points out by allusion the Âtmâ, which is *The Fourth*, the One independent of the three states. This Âtmâ can only be realized, and not meditated upon. It is for this reason that the S'ruti repeats the words " he who realizes this "

The benefit derived from this realization is that the knower himself enters into Self by means of Self. The word Âtmâ, literally translated, means Self. The knower, who having upto this time considered himself limited by one or other of the above-mentioned three conditions, now realizes that his real Self is independent of all conditions, and at this stage gives up the idea of his first limited Self, and recognises himself as the unchangeable entity free of the said conditions. The second Self into which he enters, that is to say, what he now finds himself to be, is the Âtmâ, or the Higher Self. We have shown that, Âtmâ the Higher Self, is above the senses, the mind, and the intellect, which are only the means of the attainment of knowledge. It is, therefore, very truly said that to know one's own Self (Âtmâ), no separate means are required, nor do such means have any independent existence. This is the highest end, and so the Vedas teach. The method of imparting the knowledge of Âtmâ is very unique. It is by mere allusions that Upanishads speak of that entity which is independent of all attributes, and which is above description and mental meditation. The manifestation and unmanifestation of knowledge are only different attributes qualifying the Âtmâ, and this knowledge, in both these states, being dependent for its existence on the Âtmâ, and having no separate independent existence, is comparatively considered unreal. The real and true Self of all things is truly called Âtmâ, meaning the spirit without whose support all things having a name, form and motion can never manifest themselves. This spirit is all-pervading and is not made up of parts, and is absolute; being independent of all. This Âtmâ remains unchangeable, while the different states of wakefulness, dreaminess, and sound sleep respectively appear before It. One ignorant of the independent nature of Âtmâ, qualifies *the same* with the attributes of these states, and says Âtmâ awakes, Âtmâ dreams, Âtmâ slumbers. The knowledge of unchangeableness of Âtmâ removes the fear of death, and one who realizes himself as Âtmâ, in the way spoken of in the S'rutis, becomes immortal, and secures emancipation from the misery of re-incarnation and all mortal joy and suffering.

II

EXTRACTS FROM UPANISHADS.*

WE cannot better finish this Treatise than by giving some extracts from the Vedic Literature (Upanishads), bearing on the high estimation and sanctity of the monosyllable Aum.

S'WETÂS'WATER UPANISHAD.

CHAPTER 1ST—S'RUTI 13.

13. "As the nature of fire, when concealed in its cause (the wood), is not preceived, and no destruction of its subtle body takes place since it is again (and again) preceived in its cause, the wood (by rubbing),—so it is both perceived and not perceived, in like manner the soul is perceived within the body by the sacred word (Aum)."

14. Having made his own body the lower piece of wood, and the sacred word (Aum) the upper piece, a person by abstract meditation, which serves as rubbing, will behold God, as the concealed fire becomes visible to him by rubbing.

CHAPTER 2ND—S'RUTI 8.

"Keeping the upper parts (the chest, neck, and the head) erect and even with (the other parts of) the body, subduing within the heart the senses together with the mind, let the wise, by the raft of Brahma (Aum), cross over all the fearful torrents (of the world)."

TAITTARIYA UPANISHAD—S'IKSHÂVALLI—FOURTH ANUVÂKA.

1. "May that Indra (the Supreme God in the form of Aum, the holiest word of the Vedas), who has been manifested as the

* These extracts have been taken from the Translations of the Upanishads by Dr. E. Röer and that of the Chhândogya Upanishad by Râjâ Râjendra Lâl Mitra, with very few alterations.

first of the Vedas, comprising the nature of all, being more immortal than the immortal Vedas,—strengthen me with understanding,—O God! may I be the upholder of immortality. May my body be able,—my tongue (speech) exceedingly sweet.—May I hear much with my ears. Thou (Aum) art Brahma's sheath enveloped by (common) understanding.—Preserve what (of the knowledge of Brahma) I have heard. . . . . , ..."

3. ". . . . . O Venerable! let me enter thee (Aum, the sheath of Brahma), Swâhâ.—O Venerable! do thou enter me, Swâhâ—In thee spreading in thousand branches,—O Venerable! I shall be purified, Swâhâ! . . . ."

MUNDAKA UPANISHAD—SECOND PART—SECOND SECTION.

S'rutis 3, 4 and 6.

3. "Seizing as his bow, the great weapon of the Upanishad, (let man) put (on it) the arrow, sharpened by devotion, and drawing it with the mind whose thought is fixed upon *that* (Brahma). Hit, O beloved! that indestructible (Brahma) as the aim".

4. "The sacred word "Aum" (Pranava) is called the bow, the arrow the soul, and Brahma its aim; it shall be pierced by him whose attention does not swerve. Then he will be of the same nature with him (Brahma), as the arrow (becomes one with the aim when it has pierced)."

6. "Within (the heart), which the arteries enter as the spokes do the nave of the wheel, he moves—becoming manifold. You meditate on him by the word "Aum." Let it fare-well with you, that you may cross over the sea of darkness."

KATHA UPANISHAD.—SECOND VALLI.

S'rutis 15 and 16.

15. "The seat (or word) of which all the Vedas speak, which all the works of penance proclaim, of which desirous,

they live as Brahma students, this seat I will briefly tell thee ; it is "Aum."

16. " This " Aum " is the Apara (inferior) Brahma, this "Aum" is the Para (superior) Brahma. Whoever knows this (Aum), The Immortal, obtains whatever he wishes."

PRAS'NA UPANISHAD.—FIFTH PRAS'NA.

S'RUTIS 1 TO 7.

1. " Then asked him * Satyakâmâ, the son of S'iva, which of the worlds gains he who among men has unceasingly meditated on the word "Aum" until his departure from life ? "

2. " He said to him :—O Satyakámá, the supreme (Para) and the inferior (Apara) Brahma are both the word "Aum." Hence the wise arrive by this support at one of the two."

3. " If he meditates upon one letter, being enlightened thereby, he is quickly born on the earth. . Him carry the Mantras of the Rig to the world of man. There, devoted to austerity, the duties of a Brahma student (and) faith, he enjoys greatness."

4. " Again, if he meditates in his mind on two letters (A, U), he is elevated by the Mantras of the Yajur to the atmosphere ; he (obtains) the world of the moon, he returns again (to the world of man)."

5. " Who again meditates by three letters of the word " Aum," on the Supreme Soul, is produced in light, in the sun. As the snake is liberated from the slough, so gets he liberated from sin. He is elevated by the Mantras of Sâma to the world of Brahma (Hiranyagarbha). (There) beholds the soul, that which is greater than the great totality of the

* Pippalâda Muni.

individual souls, and which is pervading (all) bodies. Here the following two memorial verses are recorded :—

6. "There are three letters, (A, U, M), subject to death, designed for the meditation of the soul, as connected or separately, they are designed for (meditation on) a special object. When the external, internal, and intermediate actions, are fully directed (to their objects), then the wise does not tremble."

7. "The wise obtains by the Mantras of the Rig this (world of man), by the Mantras of the Yajur the atmosphere (the moon), by the Mantras of the Sâma that which the sages know (as the world of Brahma), he obtains this (threefold world) by means of the word "Aum," and even the highest (Brahma) which is all calm, without decay, without death, and without fear."

BRIHAD ÂRANYAKA UPANISHAD.

5TH CHAPTER.—1ST BRÂHMANA.

"Aum" is ether, is Brahma. The ether exists of old the ether is the source of the wind, thus said the son of Kauravyâyaṇi. That (Omkara) is the Veda. The Brahmans know (Vidur) that by this (name) one knows (Veda) all that is to be known (Véditavya)."

CHHÂNDOGYA UPANISHAD.

1ST CHAPTER.—SECTION I.

1. "Om"; this letter, the Udgitha, should be adored. Om is chanted. Its description (is the following) :—

2. "The earth *constitutes* the essence of all substances; water is the essence of the earth, and herbs of water; man *forms* the essence of herbs, and speech is the essence of man; Rig is the essence of speech, Sáma of the Rig, and of the Sáma, the Udgitha (Aum) is the essence."

3. "The Udgitha is the quintessence of all these essences it is the supreme, the most adorable, the eighth."

4. "What is the Rig? What the Sáma? What the Udgitha? These are the questions."

5. "Rig is speech, Sáma is life breath, and Om, this letter is the Udgitha. Verily this and that, speech and breath (Prâna), Rig and Sáma, make a Mithuna (couple)."

6. "The Mithuna unites with the letter Om, as couples uniting together gratify each other's desires."

7. "He verily becomes the gratifier of desires, who, knowing it thus, adores the undecaying Udgitha."

8. "Verily this is an injunctive term. Whatever is enjoined, Om is surely repeated; hence this injunction is called prosperity. He verily becomes the gratifier of desires and promoter of prosperity who, knowing all this, adores the undecaying Udgitha."

9. "Through its greatness and effects is the three-fold knowledge maintained; for worship, this letter Om is recited, Om exclaimed, Om chanted."

10. "Both those who are versed in the letter thus *described*, and those who are not, alike perfom *ceremonies* through this *letter*. Knowledge and ignorance are unlike each other. What is performed through knowledge, through faith, through Upanishad, is more effectual. This verily is the description of the letter (Aum)."

Section IV.

1. "Om, this letter should be adored, Om is recited. Its description (is the following)" :—

2. "The Dévas, dreading death, adopted the three-fold knowledge of the Vedas. They shielded themselves with psalms. The psalms are called Chhandas, because the Dévas shielded (*achhádayan*) themselves therein."

3. " As *fishermen* look at fish in water, so did death behold hem in the Rig, Yajur, and Sâma hymns. They, apprised of forsaking the Vedas, of a truth betook to the asylum of he voice—Svara (Aum)."

4. " In reciting the Rig hymns, Om is articulated (Svarati), so in reciting the Yajur and Sâma; therefore, indeed, is this letter (the Udgitha), possessing immortality and safety, called Svara : Adopting its support, the Gods became immortal and secure."

5. " He who, knowing it thus, praiseth this letter, obtains the immortal and secure letter Svara ; and obtaining it, like unto the Dévas, becomes immortal."

SECTION V.

1. " Verily that which is Udgitha, is Pranava, and the Pranava (Om) is the Udgitha. The Âditya in truth is the Udgitha--the Pranava, for it moves resounding Om."

2. " Verily I sang in *praise* of the sun," said Kaushitaki to his son, " therefore have I thee alone. Know the rays and thou shalt obtain a numerous progeny." This *is the adoration of Om* as related to physical powers."

3. " Next as connected with the spirit. Verily the chief life is to be adored as the Udgitha, for, resounding Om, it proceedeth."

4. "Verily I sang in praise of that " (the chief life), said Kaushitki to his son. " Do thou sing in praise of it as manifold, praying for numerous progeny.'" "

5. " He verily, who knows the Udgitha, to be the Pranava and the Pranava to be the Udgitha, rectifies by the rituals of the Hota, the errors of the Udgâtâ,—verily rectifies the errors of the Udgâtâ."

2ND CHAPTER—SECTION XXIII.

1. "Three-fold is the division of duty. Sacrifice (Yajna), reading (of the Vedas) (Adhyayana), and charity (Dána) constitute the first ;

2. " Penance (austerity) is the second, and residence by a Brahmacharin exclusively in the house of a tutor, is the third. All those (who attend to these duties) attain virtuous regions ; the believer in Brahma alone attains to immortality."

3. " Prajâpati reflected on the (said) regions ; from them, the reflected, issued forth the three-fold knowledge ; he reflected on it : from it, the reflected, proceeded the (three) letters, Bhu, Bhuva and Sva !"

4. " On them, he reflected ; from them, the reflected, issued forth Om. As leaves are attached to their stalks, so is speech connected with Om ! Verily all this is Om ! Verily all this is Om ! "

FINIS.

Errata.

Introduction page XXVI	Line 5	for servives	read survive.
XXIX	,, 15	,, kowner	,, knower.
XXIV	,, 30	,, diciple	,, disciple.
XXXVII	,, 17	erase 'the' before we.	
XLII	,, 19	for alos	read also.
Book page 2	Line 15	for Lumnious	read Luminous.
9 & 10		for Manavantra	,, Manvantra.
27	,, 24	for Tribe	,, Tribes.
29	,, 29	,, suppossed	,, supposed.
30	,, 14	,, distininshed	,, distinguished.
30	,, 27	,, inhiretance	,, inheritance.
35	,, 1	,, panance	,, penance.
38	,, 23	,, opon	,, upon.
47	,, 4	,, preceeding	,, preceding.
47	,, 26	,, pronounciation	,, pronunciation.
55	,, 31	,, conciousness	,, consciousness.
70	,, 3	,, whosoover	,, whosoever.
70	,, 4	,, reword	,, reward.
73	,, 20	,, posses	,, possess.
74	,, 27	,, critcism	,, criticism.
75	,, 12	,, af	,, of.
77	,, 1	,, reasone	,, reasons.
78	para 84 line 2	for soleman	read solemn.
80	line 1	for anaswâra	read anuswâra.
83	,, 32	,, word	words.
85	,, 10	,, colled	called.
86	,, 13	,, contry	,, country.
92	,, 32	,, withim	,, within.
93	,, 6	,, essnece	,, essence.
74	,, 14	,, erase 'As' before Atma.	
95	,, 24	,, conditons	read conditions.
96	,, 19	,, cansonantal	,, consonantal.
96	,, 20	Insert उ before (U)	
97	,, 1	for morked	read marked.
101	,, 24	,, conciousness	,, consciousness,
108	,, 5	,, rst	First.